FLORENCE
TRAVEL GUIDE

Discover Florence's Must-see Attractions, Hidden Gems, Outdoor Activities. Practical Tips and Local Insights

JEAN Z. SCHMITZ

All rights reserved. No part of this book may be reproduced, stored in a retrieval system, or transmitted in any form or by any means, electronic, mechanical, photocopying, recording, or otherwise, without the prior written permission of the copyright owner. The information contained in this book is for general information purposes only. The author and publisher make no representations or warranties of any kind, express or implied, about the completeness, accuracy, reliability, suitability or availability with respect to the book or the information, products, services, or related graphics contained in the book for any purpose. Any reliance you place on such information is therefore strictly at your own risk.

Copyright © 2025 by Jean Z. Schmitz.

TABLE OF CONTENT

Welcome to Florence _____ 10
   Introduction to Florence _____ 10
   A Brief History of the City _____ 12
   Essential Florence Facts (language, currency, tipping etiquette, etc.) __ 14
   Florence at a Glance: _____17
   Planning Your Trip: When to Visit and How to Get There _____ 20

Top Attractions and Must-See Landmarks _____ 24
   The Duomo and Brunelleschi's Dome _____ 24
   Uffizi Gallery and the Masterpieces Within _____ 27
   Ponte Vecchio: _____ 30
   Galleria dell'Accademia and Michelangelo's David _____ 33
   Palazzo Vecchio and Piazza della Signoria _____ 36
   Basilica of Santa Croce _____ 39
   Pitti Palace and Boboli Gardens _____ 43
   Essential Tips for Visiting Florence's Landmarks _____ 46

Hidden Gems and Off-the-Beaten-Path Spots _____ 50
   Secret Passages in Palazzo Vecchio _____ 50
   Santo Spirito and the Oltrarno District _____ 53
   The Brancacci Chapel's Frescoes _____ 56
   Hidden Gardens and Quiet Courtyards _____ 59
   Artisan Workshops and Vintage Boutiques _____ 62
   Day Trips to Medieval Villages Nearby _____ 65
   Local Tips for Exploring the Unknown Florence _____ 69

Art and Culture _____ 74

- The Renaissance Revolution: 74
- Artisanal Crafts: 77
- Opera and Classical Music Venues 80
- Notable Museums Beyond the Classics 83
- Street Art and Contemporary Exhibits 87
- Seasonal Festivals and Cultural Events 90

Florentine Cuisine and Dining Experiences 94
- Classic Florentine Dishes to Try 94
- Where to Find the Best Trattorias and Osterias 97
- Street Food in Florence: 100
- Wine Tasting: 103
- Cooking Classes and Culinary Tours 107
- Markets and Local Food Producers 111
- Foodie Itineraries: A Day of Eating in Florence 114

Nightlife and Entertainment 118
- Best Bars and Wine Spots 118
- Nightclubs, Live Music, and Jazz Clubs 121
- Rooftop Views: Evening Spots with a View of Florence 124
- Theaters and Performance Spaces 127
- Seasonal Nighttime Events 130
- Tips for a Night Out in Florence 134

Shopping in Florence 138
- Fashion Boutiques and Local Designers 138
- Artisan Shops and Unique Souvenirs 141
- Leather Markets and Goldsmith Shops 144
- High-End Shops in the Historic Center 148

- Shopping Streets and Hidden Markets _____ 152
- Practical Shopping Tips for Florence _____ 155

Outdoor Activities and Nature Escapes _____ *160*

- Exploring the Boboli and Bardini Gardens _____ 160
- Walking and Hiking Trails near Florence _____ 163
- Biking Along the Arno River _____ 166
- Scenic Day Trips to Tuscany's Countryside _____ 168
- Hot Air Ballooning and Vineyard Visits _____ 172
- Picnic Spots and Panoramic Views _____ 175
- Tips for Enjoying Florence's Natural Beauty _____ 179

Suggested Itineraries _____ *184*

- Florence in One Day: _____ 184
- Florence in Two Days: _____ 187
- Florence in Three Days: _____ 190
- A Week in Florence: _____ 193
- Themed Itineraries: _____ 197
- Day Trips from Florence: _____ 201
- How to Personalize Your Own Itinerary _____ 204

Practical Information and Travel Tips _____ *208*

- Getting Around: _____ 208
- Safety Tips for Travelers _____ 211
- Budgeting for Florence: _____ 213
- Health and Wellness: _____ 216
- Accessibility Information _____ 219
- Important Numbers and Local Contacts _____ 222

Appendices and Useful Resources _____ *228*

List of Must-Have Apps for Florence Travel _____ 228

Florence's Art Movements and Influences _____ 230

Recommended Books and Films about Florence _____ 233

Conclusion _____ *238*

DISCLAIMER

Thank you for selecting our **Florence Travel Guide**! This guide is designed to provide comprehensive and insightful information about Florencei's top attractions, hidden gems, and activities. While it doesn't include images or maps, this decision is deliberate and rooted in practicality.

For navigation, real-time tools like Google Maps and similar apps are far more reliable and frequently updated, ensuring you have accurate directions and flexibility during your travels. Static maps, by contrast, can quickly become outdated and may not reflect changes or detours.

As for images, we want to inspire you to experience Florence with fresh eyes. The island's vibrant charm is best discovered in person, without preconceived notions. If you're looking for visuals, online platforms and travel apps offer dynamic and interactive options.

This guide is crafted to equip you with essential tips and insights, empowering you to create a personalized and unforgettable journey in Florence.

SCAN CODE TO VIEW MAP OF FLORENCE

Welcome to Florence

Introduction to Florence

Imagine standing on the cobblestone streets of Florence, the cradle of the Renaissance, where history, art, and culture converge in breathtaking harmony. This city, nestled in the heart of Tuscany, is more than just a destination—it's an experience that stirs the soul. Whether it's the majestic silhouette of the Duomo against a fiery sunset, the captivating brushstrokes of Botticelli's *Primavera* at the Uffizi Gallery, or the simple pleasure of a gelato enjoyed by the Arno River, Florence leaves an indelible mark on every traveler.

My first visit to Florence was a revelation. Wandering through its narrow alleys, I stumbled upon a hidden workshop in the Oltrarno district. An elderly craftsman meticulously carved delicate patterns into leather, his hands steady from decades of practice. "Florence," he said with a warm smile, "is not just to be seen; it's to be felt." And he was right. This city invites you to slow down, savor, and immerse yourself in its rich tapestry of life.

Walking through Florence feels like stepping into a living museum. The city's architectural gems tell stories of ingenuity and ambition. Take the Duomo, for instance, with Brunelleschi's audacious dome that defied engineering norms of its time. Climbing the 463 steps to the top might leave you breathless, but the panoramic view of terracotta rooftops and rolling Tuscan hills is worth every ounce of effort.

Yet, Florence isn't all grand monuments and opulent galleries. Sometimes, its magic is found in the quiet corners—a serene moment in the shadow of the Santa Croce Basilica or the soft hum of conversation at a neighborhood café. These experiences are a reminder that Florence's charm lies not only in its treasures but also in its rhythm.

While the Uffizi and Accademia are must-visits, Florence rewards the curious explorer. Venture into the Santo Spirito neighborhood, where bohemian vibes meet traditional craftsmanship. Here, you'll find lively markets, quirky boutiques, and trattorias serving *bistecca alla Fiorentina* cooked to perfection. On one occasion, I joined a group of locals for an impromptu aperitivo in Piazza Santo Spirito. With the basilica as our backdrop, we shared stories over glasses of Chianti and plates of bruschetta—a memory that remains etched in my heart.

And then there's the Oltrarno district, Florence's soul. Away from the crowds, this area feels like stepping into another era. Artisan workshops buzz with activity, and the air carries the scent of freshly baked cantucci. Don't miss the Brancacci Chapel, home to Masaccio's stunning frescoes, which quietly rival the grandeur of the city's larger attractions.

Florence is a sensory feast. The aroma of freshly brewed espresso wafts through the air as you begin your morning with a visit to the Mercato Centrale. Here, vibrant stalls overflow with fresh produce, aged cheeses, and decadent pastries. I'll never forget the vendor who insisted I try a slice of *pecorino* drizzled with honey—it was a revelation.

As the day unfolds, Florence continues to delight. Sip a spritz at a rooftop bar as the golden hour casts a magical glow over the city. For dinner, dive into the city's culinary heritage with a plate of *pappardelle al cinghiale* or savor a simple yet exquisite serving of *ribollita*, a hearty Tuscan soup.

Florence's compact size makes it a joy to explore on foot, but comfortable shoes are a must for navigating its uneven cobblestones. Mornings are the best time to visit popular landmarks before the crowds descend. And if you're here in the summer, consider an evening stroll along the Arno, when the city is bathed in a cooler, more romantic light.

For those seeking a deeper connection, join a local workshop—be it leather crafting, painting, or even a cooking class. It's an opportunity to not only take home a piece of Florence but also to experience its essence.

Florence is not a city to be rushed. It's a place where every corner holds a story, every meal is an art form, and every encounter deepens your appreciation of life's simple pleasures. So, take your time. Wander without a map, let curiosity guide you, and allow Florence to work its magic.

As you embark on this journey, this guide will be your trusted companion, offering insights, tips, and stories to enrich your experience. From iconic landmarks to hidden gems, from vibrant markets to tranquil gardens, Florence awaits. Let's begin your adventure in this timeless city.

A Brief History of the City

Florence, the capital of Tuscany, is a city that feels like it's been frozen in time—its cobblestone streets and centuries-old buildings echo with stories from the past. It wasn't always the bustling, art-filled city we know today; its transformation from a small Roman settlement to a global symbol of art, culture, and politics is nothing short of fascinating.

The Roman Beginnings:

Florence's story begins around the 1st century BC, during the time of the Roman Empire. The Romans established a settlement called *Florentia* on the banks of the Arno River. This small town was strategically positioned as a military outpost and a center for trade, with streets laid out in a typical Roman grid pattern—a layout still visible in Florence's historic center today. Walking through the Piazza della Repubblica, you can almost picture the ancient Roman forum that once stood there, with bustling merchants and traders moving through what is now a lively square.

The Middle Ages:

Fast forward a few centuries, and by the early Middle Ages, Florence had grown significantly, thanks to its position as a key trade hub in Italy. The city was ruled by powerful families, but it wasn't until the 12th and 13th centuries that Florence really began to shine as an independent republic. It was during this time that the city started to develop its own unique identity, one deeply rooted in commerce, banking, and an ever-expanding middle class.

Florence's wealth and influence grew rapidly, largely due to the establishment of the banking industry. The famous Medici family, who would later become synonymous with Florence, got their start during this period. The Medici Bank became one of Europe's most powerful financial institutions, and it was thanks to their immense wealth that Florence saw an explosion of art, architecture, and culture.

The Renaissance:

The 14th and 15th centuries marked the beginning of the Renaissance—a cultural movement that originated in Florence and would go on to change the world. Florence was at the heart of this intellectual revolution, driven by the patronage of families like the Medicis, who funded the works of some of history's greatest artists, such as Leonardo da Vinci, Michelangelo, and Botticelli.

You can trace the birth of the Renaissance in Florence to a visit to the Uffizi Gallery, where many of the masterpieces from this era are housed. The Renaissance didn't just influence art; it also brought about innovations in science, philosophy, and literature. Florence became a beacon of creativity, inspiring artists and thinkers from across Europe. The city was also home to writers like Dante Alighieri, whose *Divine Comedy* remains one of the cornerstones of Western literature.

For Florentines, the Renaissance was a time of both great pride and great challenge. The city witnessed intense political struggles, such as the rise and fall of the powerful Medici family, who alternated between being exiled and returning to power. Despite the political turmoil, the era's artistic achievements left an indelible mark on the city, from the stunning architecture of the Duomo to the iconic statue of David by Michelangelo.

Florence Under the Medici:

One of the defining chapters in Florence's history is its relationship with the Medici family. Under their rule, Florence became a cultural capital of Europe. The Medici were not only patrons of the arts but also skilled politicians, navigating the complexities of Italian city-state politics with finesse.

The family's influence is still visible today. The Palazzo Medici Riccardi, where the Medici family once lived, stands as a testament to their power, and the Uffizi Gallery, a collection built by Francesco I de' Medici, is now one of the world's premier art museums.

Florence in Modern Times:
Florence's history wasn't just shaped by artistic and political forces. In the 19th century, after a period of foreign rule, Florence became the capital of the Kingdom of Italy for a brief time, from 1865 to 1871. Though Rome eventually took the title of capital, Florence's role in shaping Italy's modern identity remains significant. In the 20th century, Florence endured the hardships of war, particularly during World War II, when it narrowly escaped being destroyed by the Nazis. Today, the scars of war are visible in some parts of the city, yet Florence's resilience shines through its continued preservation of art, culture, and heritage.

Florence Today:
Walking through Florence today, it's easy to see how the city's history has shaped its vibrant atmosphere. The same streets that once saw the Medici parading their power now welcome millions of visitors from around the world. The Renaissance may be long over, but Florence still carries its legacy proudly in the art, architecture, and local life that fill its squares and museums.

Florence is a city that invites you to explore its past while living in the present. Whether you're gazing up at the Duomo's intricate facade, sitting down for a plate of ribollita, or simply strolling through the Boboli Gardens, you're participating in the ongoing story of Florence—a city that has always celebrated creativity, resilience, and beauty.

Essential Florence Facts (language, currency, tipping etiquette, etc.)

Florence, or Firenze as the locals call it, is a city steeped in history, art, and culture. As you explore this Renaissance gem, there are a few essential facts that will help you navigate both the city and its customs with ease. Whether it's language, currency, or tips on how to blend in with the locals, here's what you should know before you go.

Language

While Italian is the official language, you'll find that many people in Florence speak at least some English, especially in tourist areas. However, a little effort to speak Italian can go a long way in making a great impression.

Though many Florentines understand English, especially in cafes or museums, using a few Italian words will make your experience feel more authentic. One personal anecdote: I once ventured into a tiny café near the San Lorenzo Market. The owner didn't speak much English, but by starting with "Buongiorno" and asking for a coffee in Italian, I was treated to a warm smile and a recommendation for a local pastry. It's these little exchanges that make Florence so memorable!

Currency

The currency in Florence is the **Euro (€)**, and credit cards are widely accepted in most places, including hotels, restaurants, and shops. However, it's always good to have some cash on hand for smaller purchases or at places that don't accept cards (like small gelato stands or local markets).

- **ATM & Currency Exchange**: ATMs are available throughout the city, and you'll find currency exchange offices in the city center, especially near major tourist attractions like Piazza del Duomo. Just make sure to check if your bank charges international withdrawal fees.

- **Tipping**: Tipping in Florence is not mandatory, but it's always appreciated for good service. Here's what you should know about tipping etiquette:
    - **Restaurants**: Most restaurants include a "coperto" (cover charge) in your bill, typically ranging from €1 to €3. This is for table setting and service. If the service has been good, rounding up the bill or leaving a tip of 5-10% is common.
    - **Bars/Cafés**: When having a coffee at a bar (such as the famous Caffè Gilli), you don't need to leave a tip, but if you're

sitting down at a table, leaving a small tip (about €1) is appreciated.

- **Taxi Drivers**: It's not necessary to tip taxi drivers, but rounding up to the nearest euro is a polite gesture.

I remember one evening at a local trattoria, after enjoying a delightful bowl of ribollita (a Tuscan soup), I rounded up my bill by a few euros. The waiter, surprised, smiled warmly and said, "Grazie mille!" (Thank you so much!). It's these simple interactions that add to the charm of Florence.

Time Zone

Florence operates in the **Central European Time Zone (CET)**, which is UTC +1 during standard time and UTC +2 during daylight saving time (usually from late March to late October). If you're coming from a different time zone, remember to adjust your schedule accordingly to avoid jet lag.

Electricity

Florence, like the rest of Italy, uses the **Type F** electrical plug, which has two round pins. The standard voltage is 230V, and the frequency is 50Hz. If you're traveling from a country with a different plug or voltage, be sure to bring an adapter and possibly a voltage converter. One tip: I once forgot my adapter, and had to scramble to find one in Florence, only to realize that local shops near the train station were well-stocked. A minor inconvenience, but it's always better to be prepared!

Public Transportation

Florence's historical center is compact and most attractions are within walking distance from each other. However, there are a few ways to get around the city if you're looking to save time or explore areas outside the center.

- **Trams and Buses**: Florence has an efficient tram and bus system, which is ideal if you're heading to more outlying areas like Fiesole or the Firenze-Santa Maria Novella Train Station. Tickets are relatively

affordable, and can be purchased at machines or tobacconists (look for the "T" sign). A single ride costs around €1.50.
- **Walking**: Florence's compact size makes walking the best way to experience the city. Take your time to stroll through its cobblestone streets, enjoy the artwork on the facades, and pop into hidden courtyards. Trust me, Florence reveals its best secrets when you take it slow.

Safety and Health
Florence is a relatively safe city for tourists, but like any popular destination, pickpocketing can occur, especially in crowded areas like the Duomo or the train station. Always keep an eye on your belongings, and use a crossbody bag or money belt to avoid any issues.

If you need medical assistance, Florence has excellent healthcare facilities, and pharmacies are easy to find. Many of them also carry over-the-counter items for minor ailments, such as cold medicine or sunscreen.

Local Customs and Etiquette
Florence is a city proud of its history and traditions, and respecting local customs goes a long way.
- **Dress Code**: When visiting churches and religious sites like the Duomo or Santa Croce, be mindful of the dress code. Cover your shoulders and knees as a sign of respect. It's not uncommon to see tourists politely turned away from entering churches in shorts or tank tops.
- **Punctuality**: Italians tend to be a bit more relaxed about time, but in general, arriving on time for tours, dinner reservations, or appointments is appreciated.

Florence at a Glance:
As the birthplace of legendary artists like Leonardo da Vinci, Michelangelo, and Botticelli, the city is a celebration of creativity and human achievement. Whether you're strolling along the Arno River or marveling at

the sculptures in the Uffizi, Florence's highlights will leave an impression that lasts a lifetime.

1. The Duomo:
The Florence Cathedral, or Duomo, is impossible to miss. Its massive, terracotta-tiled dome—designed by Filippo Brunelleschi—is an engineering marvel that dominates the city's skyline. Standing at the top of the cathedral gives you an unforgettable 360-degree view of the city, from the winding streets below to the Tuscan hills on the horizon. Climbing to the dome isn't for the faint of heart (it's 463 steps), but the breathtaking vista at the top makes the climb well worth it.
A personal anecdote: The first time I visited Florence, I hesitated to make the climb. It was a hot summer day, and the thought of climbing so many stairs seemed daunting. But once at the top, the view was nothing short of magical. The city, bathed in golden light, looked like something out of a painting. If you're up for the adventure, don't skip this experience!

2. Uffizi Gallery:
For art lovers, a visit to the Uffizi Gallery is an absolute must. Home to works by artists such as Botticelli, Leonardo da Vinci, and Raphael, this museum is one of the most important in the world. It's impossible to fully appreciate the scope of the Renaissance without stepping inside this iconic space. One of the most famous pieces here, Botticelli's *The Birth of Venus*, draws crowds from around the globe, but it's the smaller, less famous works that often make the biggest impact. Take time to linger, as the Uffizi offers a glimpse into the minds of some of the greatest artists in history. When I visited, I spent hours lost in the halls, but I found that taking breaks in the quieter corners made the experience much more enjoyable. If you're an art enthusiast, consider booking a guided tour to dive deeper into the stories behind each masterpiece.

3. Ponte Vecchio:
One of the most picturesque spots in Florence, the Ponte Vecchio (Old Bridge) spans the Arno River and is lined with charming goldsmith shops. Originally, the bridge was home to butcher shops, but now it's filled with

jewelry boutiques where you can window-shop (or splurge) on beautiful gold and silver pieces. It's a lovely spot to watch the sunset, with the bridge reflecting in the river below, creating a postcard-perfect view.
On my last visit to Florence, I found a small café by the river where I could sip a cappuccino while watching the sun set over the bridge. The atmosphere was calm and almost magical, making it the perfect way to unwind after a day of sightseeing.

4. Palazzo Vecchio and Piazza della Signoria
The Palazzo Vecchio is Florence's town hall and one of the most important buildings in the city's political history. Located in the heart of Piazza della Signoria, the palace's striking façade and imposing tower draw the eye. Inside, you'll find lavish rooms adorned with frescoes, sculptures, and tapestries that tell the story of Florence's power and wealth during the Renaissance.
But it's the piazza outside that often steals the show. The square is home to replicas of Michelangelo's *David* and Donatello's *Judith and Holofernes*, which give you a taste of the city's artistic heritage. It's a bustling, lively space, often filled with street performers, vendors, and visitors soaking in the vibrant atmosphere.

5. The Boboli Gardens:
If you're looking for a peaceful retreat from the city's hustle and bustle, head to the Boboli Gardens. Nestled behind the Pitti Palace, the gardens are a beautifully landscaped space with fountains, statues, and lush greenery. Walking through the gardens feels like stepping into a Renaissance painting, with manicured hedges and grand vistas stretching over the city. During my visit, I spent hours wandering through the winding paths, pausing to admire the views of Florence below. The gardens offer a refreshing break, and it's a great spot to have a picnic or simply relax after a day of sightseeing.

6. A Walk Through History
Walking through Florence is like walking through time. Every corner reveals something new—a hidden chapel, an ancient piazza, or a quiet lane lined

with colorful buildings. The historic center of Florence is a UNESCO World Heritage site, and it's easy to see why. The architecture, from the medieval towers to the Renaissance palaces, tells the story of the city's rich history.

Planning Your Trip: When to Visit and How to Get There

Planning your trip to Florence can be an exciting but sometimes daunting task, especially if it's your first time visiting this beautiful city. To make your experience more enjoyable, it's important to consider the best time to visit and the most efficient ways to get there. Let's dive into these two crucial aspects of your trip!

When to Visit Florence

Florence, like many Italian cities, is a year-round destination, but the time of year you choose to visit can have a big impact on your experience.

Spring (April to June)

Spring is one of the most popular times to visit Florence, and for good reason. The weather is mild, with temperatures averaging around 60-75°F (15-24°C). The city starts to bloom, and the outdoor spaces, like the Boboli Gardens, are in full display. Expect more tourists around Easter, but don't let that deter you—there are plenty of ways to enjoy Florence without feeling overcrowded. I visited in late April a few years ago and was able to enjoy less crowded streets, especially in the mornings before the crowds really began to fill up.

Summer (July to August)

If you don't mind heat and crowds, summer can still be a fun time to experience Florence. Temperatures can soar into the 90s°F (30-35°C), especially in July and August, so be prepared for the heat. Many locals escape the city for the cooler countryside during the summer, so some shops or restaurants may close for vacation, but Florence still buzzes with tourists and events. If you visit during this time, consider staying hydrated and plan for sightseeing in the early morning or later in the evening when the heat is more bearable. I remember strolling along the Arno River at sunset in late July and it was absolutely magical—the city looked like a golden painting!

Autumn (September to November)

Autumn is another fantastic time to visit Florence. The weather is cool and comfortable, and the summer crowds start to thin out. The average temperatures range from 50-70°F (10-21°C), which makes exploring the city on foot a pleasure. I visited in mid-October once, and it was one of my favorite experiences. The colors of the vineyards in Tuscany, just outside of Florence, were stunning as the leaves changed to hues of red and orange. The crowds were lighter, and the city felt more relaxed, making it easier to enjoy the sights like the Uffizi Gallery without long waits.

Winter (December to March)

If you're looking for a quieter, more intimate Florence experience, winter is your best bet. The temperatures can dip below freezing, especially in January, but Florence rarely experiences snow, so it's still quite walkable. The Christmas season is a magical time to visit, with festive decorations and markets adding to the charm. Keep in mind that some attractions may have shorter hours during this time. I once visited in early December, and while it was cold, I loved how the city felt almost like it belonged to me alone—the streets were peaceful, and there was something special about sipping a hot espresso in one of the cozy cafés after a brisk walk through the empty Piazza del Duomo.

How to Get There

Florence is well-connected to other parts of Italy and Europe, making it relatively easy to reach, whether you're traveling by plane, train, or car.

By Air
Florence's main airport is *Amerigo Vespucci Airport* (FLR), about 4 miles (6 km) from the city center. It's small but efficient, with flights coming in from major European cities like London, Paris, and Frankfurt. If you're coming from outside Europe, you might want to fly into *Pisa International Airport* (PSA), which is about an hour away by train. I flew into Pisa once and took the train to Florence—it was a scenic, comfortable ride and a good way to start my trip. Florence's airport is more convenient for short-haul flights, but Pisa's larger international connections can offer more options.

By Train
Taking the train is one of the easiest and most scenic ways to get to Florence. The city's main train station, *Firenze Santa Maria Novella* (SMN), is well-connected to cities all over Italy. If you're coming from Rome, Milan, or Venice, the high-speed trains (like *Frecciarossa* and *Italo*) will get you to Florence in 1.5 to 2 hours. I remember my first train ride from Rome to Florence; the view of the Tuscan countryside rolling by was unforgettable. Plus, trains are efficient and affordable, with frequent departures throughout the day. Once you arrive at the station, it's a short walk to many of the city's top attractions.

By Car
If you're planning to explore the Tuscan countryside as well, renting a car could be a good option. Florence is easily accessible by car from major cities like Rome (3 hours), Milan (3 hours), and Pisa (1 hour). However, be mindful that driving in Florence's historic center can be tricky—many areas are pedestrian-only zones. Parking can also be limited, so it's better to park outside the city center and use public transportation or walk. I took a road trip through Tuscany once, and it was an incredible experience, but I found that parking near the city center was a bit of a challenge.

By Bus
Traveling by bus is generally less popular than by train, but there are bus

services from many European cities. While buses are often slower, they are usually cheaper. If you're on a tight budget, this might be an option to consider, but if you're short on time, I recommend the train.

Top Attractions and Must-See Landmarks

The Duomo and Brunelleschi's Dome

This massive cathedral, with its intricate details and awe-inspiring size, stands proudly at the heart of the city. But the real showstopper is its magnificent dome – a feat of engineering and artistry that has captured the imagination of visitors for centuries. Whether you're a first-time visitor or a seasoned traveler, the Duomo and Brunelleschi's Dome are an absolute must-see.

The History of the Duomo

Before you even lay eyes on the Duomo, it's helpful to know a bit about its history. Construction began in 1296, and the cathedral was completed in 1434, but its most famous feature, the dome, wasn't finished until 1436. This is where Filippo Brunelleschi, an Italian architect and engineer, comes into the picture.

Brunelleschi was commissioned to design the dome after previous attempts to complete it had failed. His innovative design solved the problem of how to build a dome large enough to cover the cathedral without relying on traditional scaffolding. At the time, it was the largest dome in the world, and it remains one of the greatest architectural achievements of the Renaissance.

The Iconic Dome: A Marvel of Engineering

Standing beneath Brunelleschi's Dome, you can't help but be amazed by the sheer scale of the structure. The dome measures about 45 meters in diameter and towers over Florence at 114 meters high. The innovative double-shell construction of the dome allowed it to be built without external support, a truly revolutionary design for the time.

But it's not just about the engineering – the artwork inside is just as impressive. The dome is adorned with stunning frescoes depicting the Last Judgment, created by Giorgio Vasari and Federico Zuccari. As you gaze upwards, you're not just admiring the architecture, but also the skill and vision of Renaissance artists. It's a beautiful, otherworldly experience, and you'll likely find yourself standing there for a few extra moments just trying to take it all in.

Why You Should Visit the Duomo

There are so many reasons to visit the Duomo, and each visitor will find their own reason to be enchanted by it. For art lovers, it's a treasure trove of Renaissance masterpieces. For history buffs, it's a testament to the ingenuity and ambition of the time. But what makes the Duomo even more special is the sense of awe you feel when you stand before it, knowing you are experiencing a piece of Florence's rich cultural heritage.

Beyond its sheer beauty, the Duomo is an essential part of understanding Florence's historical significance. During the Renaissance, Florence was at the center of art, politics, and culture. The cathedral not only served as a place of worship but also as a symbol of the city's power and influence.

For those who appreciate architecture, standing beneath the dome is an educational experience in itself. The way it seems to float effortlessly above the city, with its intricate detailing and use of natural light, makes it a masterpiece of structural design.

What to Do at the Duomo: Activities and Tips

There's more to the Duomo than just admiring it from the outside. Here are a few activities you shouldn't miss:

1. **Climb the Dome:** If you're up for a challenge and a rewarding view, climb the 463 steps to the top of Brunelleschi's Dome. The climb is narrow and can be a bit daunting for those who aren't used to tight

spaces, but it's well worth the effort. The panoramic views of Florence are breathtaking – you'll get an incredible look at the city's rooftops, the surrounding Tuscan hills, and of course, the cathedral itself. Be sure to arrive early, as it can get crowded, especially during peak tourist season.
2. **Visit the Cathedral and Baptistery:** Don't forget to explore the cathedral itself. Step inside to see the beautifully ornate interior, the stained-glass windows, and the grand altar. The nearby Baptistery of St. John, with its golden doors (known as the Gates of Paradise), is another must-see. The interior of the Baptistery is just as stunning, with its golden mosaics gleaming above you.
3. **Explore the Museum:** The Museo dell'Opera del Duomo, located near the cathedral, is home to many of the original works of art and sculptures that once adorned the Duomo. You'll find sculptures by Donatello, Michelangelo's unfinished "Pietà," and other Renaissance masterpieces. It's the perfect way to delve deeper into the artistic and historical significance of the Duomo.
4. **Take in the Piazza del Duomo:** The piazza around the Duomo is often filled with street performers, tourists, and locals alike. It's a great spot to sit and people-watch, or simply admire the cathedral from different angles. It's especially beautiful at sunset when the golden light casts a warm glow over the façade.

Practical Information
- **Address:** Piazza del Duomo, 50122 Florence, Italy
- **Opening Hours:**
    - Cathedral: Daily 10:00 AM – 5:00 PM
    - Dome: Daily 8:15 AM – 7:00 PM
    - Museum: Daily 9:00 AM – 7:00 PM
    (Hours may vary, so it's always a good idea to check ahead)
- **Entrance Fees:**
    - Cathedral: Free
    - Dome: €20 (includes access to the Cathedral, Baptistery, Museum, and Campanile)
    - Museum: €10

- **How to Get There:**
  The Duomo is located in the historic center of Florence, so it's easy to walk to from most other central attractions. The closest bus stop is "Piazza Duomo." If you're staying nearby, it's often easiest to explore the area on foot.

Uffizi Gallery and the Masterpieces Within

When it comes to art, few places on Earth can rival the Uffizi Gallery in Florence. As one of the most famous museums in the world, the Uffizi is a must-visit for anyone with a love for Renaissance art, history, and culture. Stepping inside, you're not just visiting a gallery—you're entering a veritable time machine that transports you through centuries of masterpieces.

Address and Practical Information
Uffizi Gallery (Galleria degli Uffizi)
Address: Piazzale degli Uffizi, 6, 50122 Florence, Italy
Opening Hours:
- Monday to Sunday: 8:15 AM – 6:50 PM
- Closed on Mondays (except for special openings)
- Ticket office closes at 6:05 PM, so be sure to arrive earlier to avoid the crowds!
Website: uffizi.it

A Rich History:
The Uffizi wasn't always a museum. In fact, it began its life as a set of offices (that's what "Uffizi" means in Italian—offices) designed by Giorgio Vasari in the 16th century for Florence's ruling family, the Medici. The Medici were incredibly influential in the world of art, and over time, they transformed the building into a gallery to showcase their private art collection. By the 18th century, the Uffizi was opened to the public, cementing its status as one of Italy's top cultural institutions.

Walking through the Uffizi is like stepping through an art history textbook, with each room offering a new chapter in the evolution of European art.

Masterpieces You'll Encounter

As you wander through the Uffizi's halls, you'll encounter some of the most iconic works of art ever created. It's difficult to pick favorites, but here are a few highlights:

1. **"The Birth of Venus" by Sandro Botticelli**
   One of the most famous images in the history of art, this painting shows the goddess Venus emerging from the sea on a shell. It's not just about beauty—it's about symbolism, mythology, and Renaissance ideals. It's a work that invites awe every time you see it, and it's easy to understand why it's one of the Uffizi's most beloved masterpieces.
2. **"Annunciation" by Leonardo da Vinci**
   Leonardo's early masterpiece shows the angel Gabriel announcing to the Virgin Mary that she will bear the son of God. This piece marks Leonardo's developing genius, showcasing his attention to detail in facial expressions and the perspective of the architecture. When you stand before it, you can almost feel the stillness of the scene.
3. **"Madonna of the Goldfinch" by Raphael**
   Raphael's serene Madonna holds the Christ child with the Goldfinch perched nearby—a symbol of Christ's future suffering. Raphael's gentle portrayal of figures and his ability to capture emotion in simple gestures is what makes this work a timeless masterpiece.
4. **"The Duke and Duchess of Urbino" by Piero della Francesca**
   This beautiful portrait shows a wealthy couple gazing at the viewer. The detailed, almost photographic realism gives us a glimpse into the lives of the elite in Renaissance Italy, and the way Piero played with light and shadow makes the painting seem alive.
5. **"Tondo Doni" by Michelangelo**
   Not all of Michelangelo's masterpieces are on the ceiling of the Sistine Chapel! This stunning circular painting, depicting the Holy Family, is another example of his ability to create powerful figures and convey deep emotion through gestures and expressions.

Why You Should Visit the Uffizi Gallery

Beyond the iconic artworks, the Uffizi is a masterclass in Renaissance art. It provides visitors with a detailed look at how art evolved in Florence, from the early days of Gothic art to the full blooming of the Renaissance. For anyone with an interest in painting, sculpture, or history, this museum is an absolute must-see.

Here's why you should visit:
1. **A Journey Through Art History**
   The gallery is organized in a way that lets you see how art changed over the centuries. From the medieval period's more symbolic depictions of religious subjects to the sophisticated, humanistic portrayals of the Renaissance, the Uffizi offers a chronological walk through Italy's rich artistic heritage.
2. **Access to Iconic Works**
   Seeing paintings like *The Birth of Venus* or *The Annunciation* in person is an unforgettable experience. The colors are more vibrant, the brushwork more intricate, and the sense of history much more palpable than in any reproduction or digital version.
3. **The Architecture**
   The Uffizi itself is a work of art. Designed by Vasari, the building's graceful architecture and beautiful halls make it feel like a palace. Walking through its corridors is an experience in itself, with statues of important figures from Italian history adorning the galleries.
4. **Perfect Location**
   Situated right next to the Piazza della Signoria and overlooking the Arno River, the Uffizi is centrally located, making it easy to incorporate into your Florence itinerary. Whether you're exploring the city on foot or enjoying a coffee in one of the nearby cafés, the Uffizi is never too far away.

A Personal Experience
On my own visit to the Uffizi, I remember being struck by the sheer size of the gallery. The ceilings were high, and the walls were adorned with colorful

frames. The atmosphere was quiet, but there was a palpable sense of reverence among the visitors. I spent hours wandering from room to room, lost in the masterpieces. I especially remember the awe I felt standing in front of *The Birth of Venus*. The detail in the painting seemed almost lifelike—the waves, the texture of the sea shell—it felt as though Venus might step out of the frame at any moment.

Another great memory was the *Tondo Doni* by Michelangelo. I had always seen this image in books, but seeing it in person was a totally different experience. The way Michelangelo sculpted the figures within the painting made them appear so three-dimensional that they seemed to almost jump off the canvas.

Tips for Visiting

- **Buy Tickets in Advance**: The Uffizi is one of Florence's most visited attractions, and it can get crowded, especially in the summer months. Book your tickets online to skip the long lines.
- **Take Your Time**: You don't need to rush through the gallery. Give yourself time to take in the works and appreciate the details.
- **Guided Tours**: If you're interested in learning more about the pieces, consider joining a guided tour or using an audio guide. Many of the paintings have fascinating backstories, and a guide can help bring them to life.
- **Plan Your Visit**: With so many works to see, you might want to plan which rooms to prioritize. The Uffizi is huge, and it can be overwhelming if you try to see everything in one go.

Ponte Vecchio:

The **Ponte Vecchio**, or "Old Bridge," is perhaps the most iconic and recognizable landmark in Florence. Stretching across the **Arno River**, this medieval bridge has become a symbol of the city's rich history and vibrant culture. If you're planning a trip to Florence, it's impossible to miss this architectural gem — whether you're crossing it, shopping from its famous shops, or simply admiring its beauty from one of the many viewpoints around the city.

A Brief History of the Ponte Vecchio
The Ponte Vecchio was first constructed in **1345** by the architect **Taddeo Gaddi**, during a period when Florence was flourishing both politically and economically. The bridge was originally built to replace a previous wooden structure that had been destroyed by floods. Unlike many bridges in Europe, which were merely functional, the Ponte Vecchio was designed to be a marketplace as well, with shops lining both sides of the bridge.

Originally, these shops housed butchers, fishmongers, and other tradesmen. However, by the 16th century, the merchants were replaced by goldsmiths and jewelers, a tradition that continues to this day. It's believed that **Ferdinand I de' Medici**, the Grand Duke of Tuscany, ordered the butchers to relocate in 1593 due to the unpleasant smell, making way for the luxurious jewelry shops we see now. The Ponte Vecchio is now the only bridge in Florence that survived **World War II**, and its preservation is a testament to the resilience of the city's heritage.

What to Expect When You Visit
Address: Ponte Vecchio, 50125 Florence, Italy
You can find the Ponte Vecchio in the heart of Florence, connecting the **Pitti Palace** with the **Uffizi Gallery**. It's a quick walk from major squares like **Piazza della Signoria** and **Piazza Santo Spirito**. Whether you're on the **south side** of the Arno River (Oltrarno) or the **north side** (Centro Storico), you'll find the Ponte Vecchio to be an essential part of your journey through the city.

When you approach the bridge, you'll be greeted by its unique structure — a narrow, stone bridge with a row of colorful, wooden shops hanging over the edge, their windows filled with sparkling jewelry, gold, and silver pieces. As you walk across, you'll notice a striking panoramic view of the Arno River, flanked by centuries-old buildings. The view is even more enchanting at sunset when the soft light dances on the water.

Activities and Experiences on the Bridge
The Ponte Vecchio itself is a wonderful place to simply **stroll** and take in the sights, but there are several things you can do to enhance your experience.
1. **Shop for Jewelry:** The jewelers' shops are a major attraction on the bridge. From high-end gold pieces to exquisite silverwork and watches, you'll find a range of products. Even if you're not looking to buy, window shopping can be an enjoyable activity.
2. **Take Photos:** The views from the Ponte Vecchio are stunning. From the bridge, you can capture sweeping vistas of Florence, especially the graceful arches of the bridge itself framed against the backdrop of the city's historic buildings. If you're a photographer or just someone who loves taking memories home, this spot is a must.
3. **Walk the Vasari Corridor:** The **Vasari Corridor** is an elevated passageway that runs above the Ponte Vecchio, connecting the **Uffizi Gallery** to the **Pitti Palace**. It was created by **Giorgio Vasari** for the Medici family so they could move between their residence and the government offices without mingling with the public. Though it's not open to the public all the time, occasional tours do give you a peek at this hidden gem of Florence.
4. **Enjoy the Views of the Arno:** If you're not in the mood for shopping, just lean over the bridge and gaze at the **Arno River** below. The view of the river and its surrounding buildings is beautiful, especially in the early morning or late afternoon when the light is softer.

Why You Should Visit
The Ponte Vecchio isn't just a bridge – it's a living piece of Florence's history. For centuries, it has connected the two sides of the city, both physically and culturally. As you walk across, you are quite literally stepping in the footsteps of **Florence's past**. Whether you're admiring the medieval architecture, learning about its history, or simply enjoying the views, this bridge provides an unforgettable experience that is intrinsically linked to the city's character.

For many visitors, the Ponte Vecchio is also the perfect spot to **capture the essence of Florence** in a photograph. The shimmering gold in the windows, the reflective waters of the Arno River, and the bridge's timeworn stones create a perfect harmony that encapsulates the beauty of the city. Moreover, the **Ponte Vecchio** offers some of the best **sunset views in Florence**. If you're in town for a couple of days, make sure to return in the evening — the soft hues of the sunset over the river, combined with the twinkling lights of the shops, create a magical atmosphere.

Practical Tips for Visiting

- **Best Time to Visit:** The bridge can get quite crowded, especially in the middle of the day when tourists flood the area. Try to visit early in the morning or later in the evening if you want to avoid the crowds.
- **How to Get There:** The **Ponte Vecchio** is easily accessible from most parts of central Florence. It's a short walk from the **Piazza della Signoria** (about 5 minutes), and you can also reach it by crossing from the **Uffizi Gallery** side, or from **Piazza Santo Spirito** in the Oltrarno district.
- **Nearby Attractions:** While you're in the area, you can also visit the **Uffizi Gallery**, **Palazzo Vecchio**, or stroll through the charming streets of the **Oltrarno district**, home to artisan workshops and quieter squares.
- **Free to Visit:** Walking across the bridge is free, but if you're interested in shopping or visiting the **Vasari Corridor**, those will require a fee.

Galleria dell'Accademia and Michelangelo's David

This masterpiece has captured the admiration of art lovers for centuries and stands as a symbol of Renaissance art and Florence's rich cultural history.

Why You Should Visit

Michelangelo's *David* is not just a statue; it's a symbol of artistic perfection, of strength, and of human potential. Standing at over 14 feet tall, *David* commands the room in a way that few artworks do. When you first see it, it's almost impossible not to be struck by the sheer scale and detail of the sculpture. The marble seems to pulse with life, its contours so delicately carved that you almost expect David to step off his pedestal and move. The *David* was created between 1501 and 1504, and Michelangelo's mastery is evident in every inch of the figure. It represents the biblical hero just before he faces Goliath, with the intense focus in his eyes and the tension in his body capturing the moment of calm before the storm. Michelangelo's attention to anatomical detail was revolutionary for his time, and today *David* is widely regarded as one of the greatest sculptures ever created. But the Accademia is not just about *David*. The gallery also offers a deeper look into the world of Renaissance art, with numerous other sculptures, paintings, and fascinating works by Michelangelo and other Italian masters.

Address and Hours

The Galleria dell'Accademia is located at **Via Ricasoli, 58/60, 50122 Florence**. The museum is centrally located, just a short walk from the Duomo and other Florence landmarks.

- **Opening Hours**: The museum is typically open every day from **8:15 AM to 6:50 PM**, though it's closed on Mondays. Be sure to check the official website for any changes in opening hours or special closures, especially around holidays.
- **Ticket Prices**: Entrance costs around €12 for adults, with discounts available for students and EU citizens. It's worth noting that entry is free on the first Sunday of every month, but expect larger crowds during that time.

Activities at the Gallery

While Michelangelo's *David* is undoubtedly the star attraction, there's so much more to explore in the Galleria dell'Accademia.
1. **Michelangelo's Other Sculptures**: After you've spent time with *David*, don't miss the unfinished *Prisoners* or *Slaves* series, also by

Michelangelo. These works are fascinating for their rawness and unfinished quality. They show the artist's struggle to release the forms from the stone, offering a unique insight into his creative process.
2. **Paintings and Art Collections**: The gallery also features a stunning collection of religious paintings, including works by renowned artists such as Sandro Botticelli and Domenico Ghirlandaio. These paintings help to contextualize the Renaissance period, giving you a broader understanding of the artistic movements of the time.
3. **Music and Musical Instruments**: For a different kind of experience, the gallery also houses a collection of antique musical instruments in the museum's *Museo degli Strumenti Musicali*. This section is often overlooked by tourists, but it's a gem for anyone interested in the evolution of musical instruments throughout history.
4. **Walking Tours and Audio Guides**: To truly immerse yourself in the history and significance of the art, consider joining a guided tour or renting an audio guide. The museum's staff is knowledgeable, and a guided tour can provide a deeper understanding of the historical context behind *David* and the other works in the gallery. Audio guides are available in multiple languages and offer a flexible way to explore at your own pace.

Practical Tips for Visiting

To make the most of your visit to the Galleria dell'Accademia, here are a few tips:
- **Buy Tickets in Advance**: The *David* draws a large crowd, so it's highly recommended to buy your tickets ahead of time. Skip-the-line tickets allow you to avoid waiting in long queues, especially during the peak tourist season.
- **Visit Early**: To experience the artwork in a more peaceful setting, try to visit early in the day. The museum tends to be less crowded in the mornings, especially right when it opens.
- **Allow Time for Reflection**: Once you step into the room with *David*, take your time. The grandeur of the statue can be overwhelming, and it's worth sitting back for a moment to appreciate its scale and intricacy.

- **Combine with Other Nearby Attractions**: The Galleria dell'Accademia is located near several other Florence landmarks. After visiting, take a short walk to the nearby San Lorenzo Market for a taste of local cuisine, or head over to the nearby Duomo to explore more of Florence's architectural wonders.

A Personal Anecdote

On my first visit to the Galleria dell'Accademia, I was almost unprepared for the emotional impact of seeing Michelangelo's *David* in person. I had seen countless pictures of the statue, but nothing could compare to the experience of standing in front of it. I remember just standing there, overwhelmed by its perfection and the quiet awe that filled the room. The light coming in through the windows seemed to make the marble glow, and it felt as though I was standing in the presence of greatness. That moment has stayed with me, and I recommend taking the time to savor it, too.

Why It's Worth Your Time

The Galleria dell'Accademia is more than just a museum; it's a place to witness the pinnacle of artistic achievement. Michelangelo's *David* alone is worth the visit, but the gallery's other works and serene atmosphere will leave you with a deeper appreciation for Florence's rich cultural heritage. Whether you're an art enthusiast or a first-time visitor, the Accademia offers an unforgettable experience.

So, if you're planning a trip to Florence, make sure the Galleria dell'Accademia is on your list. Take a moment to stand in front of *David*—and let the mastery of Michelangelo and the beauty of Florence truly sink in.

Palazzo Vecchio and Piazza della Signoria

Whether you're a history buff or someone who enjoys exploring grand, historical landmarks, this pair is a must-visit during your time in Florence. Let's dive into what makes these iconic sites so captivating and why they should be at the top of your Florence itinerary.

Piazza della Signoria:
Located at the very center of Florence, Piazza della Signoria is more than just a public square—it's a historic symbol of political power, art, and culture. For centuries, it has been the city's main political center, hosting the **Florentine Republic's government** and serving as a stage for important public events, such as executions and celebrations. Today, it remains a bustling gathering place for locals and tourists alike, surrounded by world-class art and history.

Address: Piazza della Signoria, 50122 Firenze, Italy
Opening Hours: The square is open 24 hours, but most attractions around it have specific hours.

As you enter the square, the **Palazzo Vecchio** looms over you on one side, and it's impossible to ignore its striking appearance. But before heading into the palace, take a moment to appreciate the outdoor sculptures scattered across the square. The **Statue of Neptune**, **The Fountain of the Sculptures**, and perhaps the most famous of all, **Michelangelo's David** (a replica, as the original resides in the Galleria dell'Accademia), stand proudly amidst the hustle of the square. These statues, coupled with the square's bustling cafes and street performers, create an atmosphere that's rich with both art and life.

For a more immersive experience, take a seat at one of the nearby cafes and people-watch while soaking in the square's energy. The atmosphere in Piazza della Signoria can shift depending on the time of day—early mornings are peaceful, while afternoons and evenings see crowds gathering to admire the works of art or to catch a performance in the square.

Palazzo Vecchio: Florence's Medieval Powerhouse

The **Palazzo Vecchio**, or "Old Palace," is the centerpiece of Piazza della Signoria. Built in the late 13th century, this fortress-like palace has served as Florence's town hall for over 700 years and has seen history unfold within its walls, from the rule of the **Medici family** to the Renaissance's most iconic events.

Address: Piazza della Signoria, 50122 Firenze, Italy
Opening Hours: Monday-Sunday: 9:00 AM - 7:00 PM
Entry Fee: Adults - €12, Reduced - €8.50

As you approach the grand entrance, the impressive **Torre d'Arnolfo** (the bell tower) reaches towards the sky, offering a perfect photo op. Visitors can climb the 223 steps to the top for panoramic views of Florence, which are especially breathtaking at sunset. From the tower, you'll catch a glimpse of the entire city, from the Duomo to the hills of Tuscany.

Once inside, the **Palazzo Vecchio** is a journey through time. The rooms are filled with **Renaissance-era frescoes**, **statues**, and intricate **furniture**—each one a reflection of the city's artistic and political significance during the Medici's reign.

One of the most renowned spaces within the palace is the **Salone dei Cinquecento** (Hall of the Five Hundred), a vast room adorned with murals that tell the story of Florence's political history. This was once the meeting place for the **Florentine Council**, and it is still used for official events today. If you're lucky, you might catch a glimpse of a live event or performance hosted in this iconic room.

For art lovers, the **Palazzo Vecchio** also features works by **Giorgio Vasari** and **Michelangelo**, as well as a series of intriguing exhibits about the Medici family's rule and Florence's fascinating past.

One of my personal favorite parts of visiting the Palazzo is the **secret passages**—hidden corridors that were used by the ruling family to move discreetly around the palace. It's like stepping back in time to imagine what it was like to live in such a political powerhouse, always keeping an eye out for intrigue and scandal.

Why You Should Visit

If you're wondering whether a visit to **Palazzo Vecchio** and **Piazza della Signoria** is worth your time, the answer is undoubtedly yes. These sites are not only landmarks of Florence's **Renaissance** history but also places where you can feel the pulse of the city. The **Palazzo Vecchio** is a treasure trove of art and history, while **Piazza della Signoria** offers the perfect mix of outdoor beauty, art, and Florence's vibrant public life.

When you're here, you're not just seeing a building or a square—you're stepping into the heart of Florence's political past and experiencing the essence of what makes this city so special. Whether you're marveling at the **statues**, climbing the tower for panoramic views, or getting lost in the ornate rooms of the palace, every moment here feels like an invitation to dive deeper into the city's soul.

Practical Tips

- **Best Time to Visit:** If you want to avoid the crowds, visit early in the morning or later in the evening when the square is less busy. The evening light also casts a beautiful glow on the building facades and statues.
- **Combine with Other Attractions:** The **Uffizi Gallery** is just a short walk away, so plan to visit both in one day. If you're feeling adventurous, consider heading to the **Piazzale Michelangelo** afterward for even more stunning views of Florence.
- **Guided Tours:** For a deeper understanding of the history and art within the **Palazzo Vecchio**, I recommend taking a guided tour. The stories behind the artworks and the political drama are fascinating!

Basilica of Santa Croce

Nestled in the heart of the city, this stunning church is not only a masterpiece of Gothic architecture, but also a vibrant symbol of Florence's rich cultural and religious history. It's a place where art, history, and spirituality come together, offering visitors an unforgettable experience.

Address and Practical Information

The **Basilica of Santa Croce** is located at **Piazza di Santa Croce, 16, 50122 Florence, Italy**. You can easily reach it by walking from the city center, as it is just a short stroll from the **Piazza della Signoria** and the **Uffizi Gallery**, making it an ideal stop on any Florence itinerary. The church is open every day from **9:30 AM to 5:30 PM** (with extended hours during special events), and the entrance fee is typically **€8**. For those interested in exploring more of its treasures, an audio guide or guided tour is available for a richer, more immersive experience.

Why You Should Visit Santa Croce

1. **Home to Iconic Tombs**: One of the most compelling reasons to visit the **Basilica of Santa Croce** is its incredible collection of tombs of some of Italy's most famous figures. As you step inside, you'll notice the grandeur of the tombs dedicated to renowned artists, scientists, and political figures, including **Michelangelo, Galileo Galilei, Niccolò Machiavelli**, and **Giorgio Vasari**. Each tomb is a work of art in itself, designed with reverence and respect for the individuals they commemorate.

I remember my first visit to the church, standing in front of **Michelangelo's tomb** and marveling at the sheer scale of the monument. It felt surreal to be so close to the final resting place of one of the greatest minds in history. As a Florence resident, I often take a moment to reflect on the genius that passed through this city, and Santa Croce offers the perfect setting for such contemplation.

2. **The Art of the Church**: The Basilica is a masterpiece of Gothic architecture, with its **stunning frescoes**, intricate **stonework**, and high vaulted ceilings. As you explore the church, you'll be drawn to the **frescoes by Giotto** and his school, which depict scenes from the lives of Christ and the Virgin Mary. These frescoes are not just religious

works; they are a window into the artistic vision of the time, showing how art and religion intertwined to tell the stories of faith.

I'll never forget the first time I saw **Giotto's "The Crucifixion"** — the emotion conveyed through the figures and the use of light was so striking that it almost felt as if the scene was coming to life before my eyes. It's one of those experiences that remind you of the transformative power of art, and Santa Croce is full of these moments.

3. **A Spiritual Retreat**: Beyond the art and history, the Basilica of Santa Croce is also a place of quiet contemplation. The church is the burial site of the **Franciscan Order**, which means you're walking through a space that holds centuries of spiritual significance. There's something special about sitting quietly in the pews, surrounded by the towering arches and the soft light filtering through the stained-glass windows. For anyone seeking a moment of peace amidst the bustling city, Santa Croce offers a serene environment for reflection or simply absorbing the beauty around you.

4. **The Cloisters and the Museum**: If you have the time, don't miss the **Cloisters of Santa Croce** and the **Museum**. The peaceful cloisters are a perfect place for a stroll, offering a calm contrast to the lively piazza outside. The museum houses some of the church's most important art collections, including **early Christian relics**, **tapestries**, and **liturgical objects** that tell the story of Florence's religious and artistic evolution. If you're interested in Florence's history beyond the popular tourist sites, this museum is a hidden gem.

Activities and Things to See
- **Attend a Mass or Concert**: While most tourists visit the church for its art and history, the Basilica of Santa Croce also offers a spiritual experience through its regular **masses and concerts**. Florence's grand churches often host classical music performances, and the acoustics of Santa Croce make it an exceptional venue for this. If you time your visit right, you might

have the chance to experience a concert within the beautiful walls of this sacred space.
- **Guided Tours**: To get the most out of your visit, consider taking a **guided tour**. Guides can provide fascinating insights into the church's art, architecture, and history. I once joined a tour where the guide shared stories about the tombs of **Machiavelli** and **Galileo**, and it truly brought the history of these figures to life in a way that I hadn't experienced on my own.
- **Visit the Leather Market**: Just a short walk away from Santa Croce is **Florence's leather market**, a great place to pick up unique souvenirs. Whether you're looking for high-quality leather goods, jewelry, or other artisan crafts, this bustling market offers plenty of options. I always enjoy wandering through and browsing the beautifully crafted bags, belts, and jackets made from Florentine leather.

Why Santa Croce Stands Out

The Basilica of Santa Croce is more than just a beautiful church. It's a place where you can feel the pulse of Florence's history, from its Renaissance glory to the modern-day reverence for art and faith. Whether you're an art lover, a history buff, or someone seeking a quiet spot to reflect, Santa Croce offers something for everyone.

It's easy to get caught up in the more famous attractions like the **Uffizi Gallery** and the **Duomo**, but if you want to experience Florence in a more intimate and thought-provoking way, the **Basilica of Santa Croce** is the perfect place to explore.

Whether you're admiring **Giotto's frescoes**, reflecting on the tombs of great Italians, or simply soaking in the beauty of the church's architecture, you'll find that this space leaves a lasting impression.

Pitti Palace and Boboli Gardens

When you visit Florence, it's easy to get caught up in the well-known art galleries and architectural landmarks. But sometimes, the most memorable experiences come from places that let you step back in time, and few places do this better than the **Pitti Palace** and the adjoining **Boboli Gardens**. These two gems offer a perfect blend of history, art, and outdoor beauty, all within walking distance from the Ponte Vecchio.

The Pitti Palace:

Located on the **south side of the Arno River**, just a short walk from the city center, the **Pitti Palace** (Palazzo Pitti) is a massive Renaissance palace that once served as the residence of the powerful Medici family, one of Italy's most influential dynasties. Today, the palace is a museum complex housing several galleries, each showcasing remarkable works of art, decorative arts, and fashion.

The palace itself is a magnificent example of Renaissance architecture. The **Pitti Palace** was originally built for Florentine banker Luca Pitti in 1458, but its grandeur was expanded when the Medici family took ownership in 1549. If you're a fan of art history, stepping into the palace feels like you're walking through the pages of a history book.

Once you enter, you'll find yourself surrounded by **paintings, sculptures, and period furniture**, much of it from the Medici's personal collection. You can visit the **Palatine Gallery**, where you'll be stunned by works from the likes of Raphael, Titian, and Rubens. It's a treasure trove for art lovers, and what makes it special is the sense of intimacy—these pieces were once in the very rooms where the Medici family lived. It's as if you're walking through a living museum.

One of the most fascinating parts of the **Pitti Palace** is the **Royal Apartments**. These rooms, still decorated in their original splendor, allow you to imagine what life was like for the grand ducal family of Tuscany. The rooms are a mix of opulent furnishings, grand mirrors, and intricate woodwork that reflect the wealth and power the Medici once held.

Boboli Gardens:

After soaking in the palace's impressive history and artwork, it's time to explore the sprawling grounds of the **Boboli Gardens**. The gardens are located directly behind the Pitti Palace and are an integral part of the complex. They are one of Italy's finest examples of **Italian garden design**, blending art, nature, and design in a way that offers a peaceful escape from the hustle and bustle of the city.

Walking through the Boboli Gardens feels like stepping into another world. The gardens cover **45,000 square meters**, so you'll definitely get your steps in. The layout is full of wide, grassy spaces, well-manicured hedges, statues, fountains, and grottos, all set against the backdrop of the Tuscan hills. It's easy to lose track of time here, wandering through tree-lined paths and stopping to admire the occasional marble statue.

One of the most iconic spots in the gardens is the **Isolotto**, a small island in a pond with a striking statue of **Oceanus** at its center. It's a popular spot for photos, and the reflections in the water add to the allure.

As you explore, be sure to head to the **Porcelain Museum**, which is housed in a small building within the gardens. This museum, though often overlooked, is home to a remarkable collection of European porcelain, dating back to the 18th century. It's a hidden gem that offers a unique cultural perspective beyond the usual art museums.

The gardens also feature a number of **terraces and viewpoints** that offer stunning panoramic views of Florence. If you make it to the top, you'll be rewarded with a breathtaking view of the entire city, with the Duomo and the hills surrounding Florence. It's the perfect spot for a break, perhaps with a gelato in hand, and a moment to take it all in.

Why You Should Visit the Pitti Palace and Boboli Gardens
1. **A Step into History**: For anyone interested in Renaissance Florence and the Medici family, the **Pitti Palace** offers a rare opportunity to experience life through their eyes. You're not just admiring art and architecture; you're stepping into the grandeur of a bygone era. I'll never forget the feeling of walking through the royal apartments, imagining the Medici family hosting lavish gatherings in the very rooms I was standing in.
2. **Art and Nature Combined**: Few places combine art, history, and nature as seamlessly as the Pitti Palace and Boboli Gardens. After soaking in centuries of artwork, stepping out into the gardens provides a perfect way to unwind and enjoy the beauty of Florence from a different angle.
3. **The View**: If you want the best view of Florence, make sure to hike up to the highest point of the Boboli Gardens. From there, you'll get one of the most picturesque vistas of the city, with the Arno River winding through the heart of Florence, and the Duomo in the distance.
4. **A Family-Friendly Experience**: Whether you're traveling solo, as a couple, or with family, both the **Pitti Palace** and the **Boboli Gardens** offer something for everyone. Kids can enjoy the wide-open spaces of the gardens, while adults can marvel at the art in the palace.
5. **A Peaceful Escape**: One of the most underrated aspects of visiting the Boboli Gardens is the peace and quiet it offers. Despite being a popular tourist spot, the size of the gardens allows you to find quieter corners where you can relax and enjoy the natural beauty.

Practical Information
- **Address**: Piazza de' Pitti, 1, 50125 Florence, Italy
- **Opening Hours**:
    - **Pitti Palace**: 8:15 AM - 6:50 PM (closed Mondays)
    - **Boboli Gardens**: 8:15 AM - 6:30 PM (closed Mondays)
- **Admission**:
    - **Pitti Palace**: €16 for full access (Palatine Gallery, Royal Apartments, Modern Art Gallery, and Treasury of the Grand Dukes)
    - **Boboli Gardens**: €10 (or included in the Pitti Palace ticket)

- **How to Get There**: The Pitti Palace is easily accessible from the city center. It's about a 10-minute walk from the Ponte Vecchio. You can also take the **bus** or walk along the Arno River for a scenic approach.

Essential Tips for Visiting Florence's Landmarks

Whether you're gazing up at the Duomo or strolling along the Arno River, you'll encounter architectural wonders and timeless art that have shaped the city for centuries. But as with any major tourist destination, there are a few insider tips that can make your visit smoother, more enjoyable, and even more rewarding. So let's dive into some essential advice that will help you navigate Florence's most famous landmarks like a pro.

1. Plan Your Visits in Advance

Florence's landmarks, like the **Duomo**, the **Uffizi Gallery**, and **Piazza della Signoria**, are world-renowned, which means they can get crowded, especially during peak tourist season (May to September). If you're aiming to explore these sites at a leisurely pace, booking tickets in advance is a smart move. For example, the **Uffizi Gallery** often has long lines, but by reserving a time slot online, you can skip the queues and spend more time soaking in the incredible masterpieces inside.

I've learned the hard way that arriving right when a museum or site opens can make a huge difference. On one trip, I went to the **Galleria dell'Accademia** (home to Michelangelo's David) early in the morning and had the entire gallery almost to myself for the first half hour. It was surreal to stand inches away from David without having to jostle for space!

2. Dress Comfortably and Appropriately

Florence is a city meant to be explored on foot, so comfortable shoes are essential. Whether you're tackling the long staircase up to the **Duomo's dome** or wandering through the cobbled streets of the historic center, you'll want something sturdy. Avoid wearing sandals with flimsy soles—trust me, your feet will thank you.

Additionally, many of Florence's churches and religious sites, such as **Santa Croce** and the **Basilica of San Lorenzo**, require modest dress. If you're planning on visiting religious landmarks, be sure to cover your shoulders and knees. A light scarf or shawl can be a lifesaver when it comes to dressing appropriately.

3. Take Time to Explore the Hidden Corners

While Florence's main attractions are undoubtedly impressive, don't rush past the quieter, hidden gems that make the city so special. For instance, the **Boboli Gardens** (located behind the **Pitti Palace**) offer stunning views over Florence, and you can escape the crowds here while still enjoying beautiful landscapes and sculptures. I've had afternoons in the gardens where I was almost alone, making it the perfect spot to take a break from the hustle of the city.

Another hidden gem is the **Bargello Museum**—a quieter, less crowded alternative to the Uffizi. It houses incredible sculptures from Renaissance masters like Donatello and Michelangelo, and the serene environment allows for a more relaxed, intimate experience with the art.

4. Time Your Visits for the Best Experience

Timing is crucial for a fulfilling experience in Florence. Many of the most popular landmarks, such as the **Duomo** and **Ponte Vecchio**, can get swamped by mid-afternoon. If you're planning to visit the **Duomo**, it's worth noting that the earlier you go, the better your chance of seeing the cathedral and climbing the dome without feeling rushed.

If you're visiting during the summer, be mindful of the heat. The sun can be intense in Florence, especially in August, so try to schedule outdoor activities like a walk through **Piazza della Signoria** early in the morning or late in the evening. Midday is a great time to enjoy the cool, shaded interiors of Florence's museums, galleries, and churches.

5. Take Advantage of Florence's City Passes

If you're keen on seeing multiple landmarks, consider purchasing a **Florence Museum Pass** or a **Firenze Card**. These passes offer skip-the-line access to top attractions and can be more economical if you plan to visit several places during your trip. For example, the **Firenze Card** grants access to more than 70 museums and monuments, including the **Uffizi**, **Pitti Palace**, and **Accademia**, with the added benefit of skipping long lines.

In my experience, the card was particularly useful for a short trip, allowing me to see the major landmarks without the stress of waiting in lines. However, be mindful that some popular sites, like the **Uffizi**, may still require a reservation for timed entry, so always double-check.

6. Take a Guided Tour for Deeper Insights

Florence is rich in history and culture, and sometimes a little expert insight can transform your visit from a standard sightseeing tour to an unforgettable journey. Whether you're interested in art, history, or architecture, a knowledgeable guide can give you context and interesting anecdotes that bring the landmarks to life.

I joined a walking tour of **Piazza della Signoria** one afternoon, and the guide shared fascinating details about the sculptures and their symbolic meanings that I never would have learned on my own. Additionally, a tour often leads to smaller, lesser-known places that you might miss if you're exploring independently.

7. Don't Miss the View from Piazzale Michelangelo

While visiting the **Piazzale Michelangelo** isn't quite a "landmark" in the traditional sense, it's definitely a must-see for anyone in Florence. From this panoramic viewpoint, you can get an amazing, sweeping view of the city, including the **Duomo**, **Ponte Vecchio**, and the Arno River. It's particularly breathtaking at sunset.

For an extra tip: skip the bus and walk up the hill from the city center. It's a bit of a climb, but the journey up is part of the experience. You'll be rewarded with an even better view and a sense of accomplishment!

8. Why You Should Visit Florence's Landmarks

Visiting Florence's landmarks is not just about checking off a list of famous sites. It's about stepping into a world that shaped the course of art, culture, and architecture. From the stunning **Florence Cathedral** with its signature dome to the **Uffizi Gallery**, home to works by Botticelli and Leonardo da Vinci, each site tells the story of human achievement and creativity. Florence's landmarks allow you to connect with the Renaissance in a personal way, experiencing it not just through textbooks, but through the very streets, buildings, and artworks that defined an era.

Hidden Gems and Off-the-Beaten-Path Spots

Secret Passages in Palazzo Vecchio

The Palazzo Vecchio, Florence's iconic town hall, is more than just a stunning piece of Renaissance architecture. Beyond its grand façade and celebrated art, it hides an intriguing secret: a network of hidden passages and rooms that give us a glimpse into the private world of the powerful Medici family. These secret spaces are a testament to Florence's rich political history and its cultural legacy.

Why Visit the Secret Passages?
While the grand halls and galleries of Palazzo Vecchio are awe-inspiring, it's the hidden corners that tell the most fascinating stories. These secret passages served not only as a way for the Medici to move undetected throughout the palace but also as a method of political maneuvering. The Medici, often embroiled in political intrigue, used these concealed corridors to escape danger, conduct private meetings, and ensure their safety in the face of their many enemies.

A visit to the secret passages offers a unique opportunity to step into a world that's been carefully preserved, giving you a peek into the lives of Florence's most powerful family. These hidden spaces also provide an escape from the crowds and allow you to experience a quieter, more intimate side of the city's rich history.

Exploring the Secret Passages
The most famous of the secret passages in Palazzo Vecchio is the **"Corridoio Vasariano,"** or Vasari Corridor. Named after Giorgio Vasari, the renowned architect and artist, this corridor was built in 1565 to connect Palazzo Vecchio with the Pitti Palace across the river. It allowed the ruling family to

move between their government headquarters and their residence without ever stepping foot in the streets of Florence—effectively avoiding public scrutiny.

The Vasari Corridor is a remarkable work of art in itself. Stretching over a kilometer, it's adorned with portraits of Tuscan rulers and powerful figures from Florence's history. The passageway also offers beautiful views of the Arno River and the Ponte Vecchio, but the real thrill comes from walking in the footsteps of history and imagining the secrets it held.

One of the most fascinating aspects of the passage is how it was designed for secrecy. While it may appear like a simple corridor today, it once had many concealed doors and hidden windows that allowed for surveillance of the street below. These features were crucial for the Medici family's protection from potential threats, as well as for maintaining their sense of power and control over the city.

How to Visit the Secret Passages
If you're eager to explore these hidden corners of Palazzo Vecchio, you'll need to book a special guided tour. The secret passages are not accessible to visitors during regular tours, as they are not part of the main palace route. However, with a special reservation, you can join one of the guided tours that give you exclusive access to these mysterious spaces.

The tours typically last about 90 minutes and will take you through some of the palace's most private areas, including the Vasari Corridor. Along the way, your guide will share fascinating anecdotes and historical details, helping you uncover the Medici's political machinations, their private lives, and how these corridors played a key role in their legacy.

Address: Palazzo Vecchio, Piazza della Signoria, 50122 Florence, Italy
Opening Hours: 9:00 AM - 7:00 PM (varies depending on season)
Admission: General entry is free for residents and members, but access to the secret passages requires booking a special tour. Expect to pay between €20 and €40 per person for a guided tour.

Activities: Guided tours, exploring the Vasari Corridor, learning about Renaissance politics, and seeing hidden treasures.

Why You Should Visit:
- **Historical Significance**: Step into the Medici family's shoes and explore a part of the palace few visitors get to see.
- **Exclusive Experience**: The secret passages aren't included in regular entry, so this is a more intimate and personalized way to experience Palazzo Vecchio.
- **Art and Architecture**: As you walk through the passages, enjoy artwork, portraits, and architectural details not visible to the general public.
- **Unique Perspective**: See Florence from a different angle, as the secret passages provide stunning, often overlooked views of the city.

Personal Anecdotes and Insider Tips

During my own visit to Palazzo Vecchio, I was fortunate enough to book one of the secret passage tours. I'll never forget the moment when we stepped into the dimly lit corridor, its walls lined with portraits and ancient frescoes. The guide, a historian with a deep knowledge of Florence's political history, shared stories of the Medici family's tactics for avoiding assassination attempts. It felt like stepping into a spy novel!

One of the most remarkable parts of the tour was seeing the window that overlooked the **Ponte Vecchio**. From here, the Medici could keep an eye on their rivals while remaining out of sight. It was like stepping back in time, witnessing the blend of art, politics, and power that shaped Florence's destiny.

Practical Advice:
- Book your tour in advance, especially during peak tourist season, as spots can fill up quickly.
- Bring comfortable shoes, as the tour involves a fair amount of walking and some stairs.

- Don't rush through the passages; take time to appreciate the artworks and historical details along the way.
- If you're keen on photography, check with your guide beforehand to see if photos are allowed in the corridors.

Santo Spirito and the Oltrarno District

If you're looking to experience the authentic, unpolished side of Florence, head across the Arno River to the **Oltrarno District**, where you'll find **Santo Spirito**, a lively neighborhood that still retains its traditional charm and local vibe. This area, often overlooked by tourists, offers a delightful contrast to the more famous, crowded sights on the north side of the river. Here's why you should make time to explore it.

Santo Spirito:
The heart of the Oltrarno is the **Basilica di Santo Spirito**, a stunning church designed by Filippo Brunelleschi, the mastermind behind the Duomo's dome. While not as famous as its counterpart across the river, this church is a gem in its own right, with a beautiful interior featuring simple yet striking design elements that showcase the elegance of Renaissance architecture.

Address: Piazza Santo Spirito, 50125 Florence
Opening Hours: Monday to Saturday, 9:00 AM – 1:00 PM, 4:00 PM – 7:00 PM (Closed Sundays)
Entry Fee: €5 (free for residents of Florence)

The church's most notable feature is its peaceful ambiance, providing a calming atmosphere that contrasts with the bustling city. The altarpiece, which depicts the Virgin Mary with Saints, is particularly impressive, and the church also houses some works by renowned artists like Filippino Lippi.

Walking through the church, you'll notice how much quieter and more contemplative it feels compared to the crowds at the Duomo. It's a great place to take a break and reflect, giving you a moment of tranquility amidst the energy of Florence.

Exploring the Oltrarno District

The Oltrarno District itself is full of life and character, with narrow cobblestone streets, lively piazzas, and hidden courtyards. It's a neighborhood where locals go about their daily lives, and it's one of the few places left in Florence where you can still experience that authentic Italian atmosphere.

One of the best ways to explore the Oltrarno is simply by wandering. Meander down Via Romana, a charming street lined with traditional workshops selling leather goods, ceramics, and other artisan creations. Here, you'll find small boutiques where you can pick up unique souvenirs that are handcrafted by local artisans, often in their own studios.

In the evenings, the streets come alive with Florentines socializing in the cafes, bars, and trattorias that line the squares. The **Piazza Santo Spirito** is especially lively at night, often filled with locals enjoying a drink or chatting at outdoor tables. It's a great spot to people-watch and soak in the atmosphere of the neighborhood.

Artisans and Handcrafted Goods
One of the reasons the Oltrarno is so beloved by Florentines is its thriving artisan community. The area is home to some of the best workshops in the city, where you can watch craftsmen create everything from handmade leather goods to intricate jewelry.

I remember walking into a small leather shop one afternoon where I met a skilled artisan who was crafting a beautiful wallet by hand. She explained the entire process to me, from choosing the right kind of leather to stitching it together by hand. I ended up buying a wallet that's still one of my favorite keepsakes from Florence. Experiences like this—where you get to witness the artistry behind the product—are what make the Oltrarno so special.

The **Via de' Serragli** street is particularly known for its workshops and galleries. If you're interested in purchasing a handmade souvenir or perhaps learning a craft yourself, you'll find many studios offering hands-on workshops in everything from bookbinding to painting.

Pitti Palace and Boboli Gardens

The **Pitti Palace**, another must-see in the Oltrarno, is a Renaissance-era palace once home to the powerful Medici family. Now a complex of museums, it houses an impressive collection of Renaissance art, royal furnishings, and much more. But what makes the palace truly unique is its stunning **Boboli Gardens**, which are just as much of an attraction as the palace itself.

The gardens are a peaceful retreat where you can take a leisurely stroll under the shade of ancient trees, discover hidden fountains, and enjoy sweeping views of the city. I visited Boboli Gardens during spring, and the flowers were in full bloom, adding to the enchantment of the place. It's one of those spots where you can lose yourself for hours, all while being surrounded by beauty and history.

Address: Piazza de' Pitti, 1, 50125 Florence
Opening Hours: 8:15 AM – 6:30 PM (check for seasonal changes)
Entry Fee: €10 (combined ticket with Pitti Palace)

Why You Should Visit the Oltrarno

There are many reasons to visit the Oltrarno, but the biggest draw is its authenticity. While the north side of Florence may have its famous attractions, the Oltrarno offers something different: a quieter, more laid-back experience where you can engage with Florence's local culture. Here, you can visit historic sites without the crowds, enjoy incredible local food, and discover unique artisan shops where your purchases help support the local economy.

For anyone seeking a deeper, more personal connection to Florence, the Oltrarno district offers a slower, more intimate pace. You'll leave with memories of friendly interactions, breathtaking views, and a sense of having truly connected with the soul of Florence.

The Brancacci Chapel's Frescoes

Nestled within the stunning **Santa Maria del Carmine** church in Florence, the **Brancacci Chapel** is a must-visit for art lovers and history enthusiasts alike. While it may not be as widely known as the Uffizi or the Duomo, this small but magnificent chapel holds some of the most significant frescoes of the Renaissance period. If you're planning to immerse yourself in Florence's rich artistic heritage, the Brancacci Chapel offers a unique and intimate glimpse into the past, making it a hidden gem worth exploring.

A Brief History of the Brancacci Chapel

The Brancacci Chapel was commissioned in the early 15th century by **Felice Brancacci**, a wealthy Florentine merchant, and is renowned for its frescoes that tell the biblical story of **St. Peter**. The chapel was painted by **Masaccio, Masolino da Panicale**, and later, **Filippo Lippi**, among others, and the frescoes are considered pivotal in the development of Western art. Masaccio's work, in particular, revolutionized art with his use of perspective, light, and shadow, contributing to the move away from the medieval style toward the more naturalistic Renaissance approach.

What You'll See Inside the Chapel

As soon as you step into the Brancacci Chapel, you'll be immediately struck by the vibrancy and emotion that radiate from the frescoes. The chapel's fresco cycle portrays scenes from the life of **Saint Peter**, including his **denial of Christ, the healing of the crippled man**, and the **call of St. Peter**. These images are filled with dynamic figures and bold colors, showcasing Masaccio's groundbreaking use of **perspective** and **chiaroscuro** (the treatment of light and shadow). His revolutionary approach is most evident in the **Expulsion of Adam and Eve from Eden**, a striking and emotionally raw scene that exemplifies his masterful skill in conveying human emotion.

While Masaccio's contributions to the frescoes are the most famous, the chapel also includes work by his contemporaries, such as **Masolino**'s **Temptation of Adam and Eve**, which contrasts with Masaccio's more dramatic style. The differences between their styles make the chapel a fascinating study in the evolution of Renaissance art. But the real star of the show is **Masaccio's The Tribute Money**, one of the most celebrated frescoes in the world. This work not only illustrates a biblical story but also highlights Masaccio's genius in creating realistic space and depth, something that would set the stage for the entire Renaissance.

Why You Should Visit the Brancacci Chapel

One of the key reasons to visit the Brancacci Chapel is its unparalleled artistic significance. It is often considered the "Sistine Chapel" of the early Renaissance. For anyone passionate about art, the chapel offers an intimate opportunity to study Masaccio's innovative work up close, without the overwhelming crowds that often accompany Florence's more famous sites.

As you stand before Masaccio's frescoes, you're walking through a story—one that blends religious themes with revolutionary artistic techniques. It's a chance to see firsthand how artists of the Renaissance transitioned from the flat, symbolic styles of the Middle Ages to a more lifelike and emotional representation of the human experience. The chapel offers a perfect snapshot of how art changed the course of history.

Another reason to visit the Brancacci Chapel is its location. While it may be slightly off the beaten path, it's easily accessible and allows you to experience a quieter, less tourist-heavy side of Florence. The **Santa Maria del Carmine** church is located in the **Carmine district** of Florence, a charming area that's rich in local culture. After exploring the chapel, you can take a leisurely stroll through the nearby streets and enjoy the authentic Florence that locals love. You might even discover a quaint café or artisan shop tucked away in a corner.

Address, Hours, and Admission

Address:
Santa Maria del Carmine, Piazza del Carmine, 14, 50124 Florence, Italy

Hours:
The chapel is typically open daily, though hours may vary, so it's a good idea to check in advance. Most days, it's open from **10:00 AM to 6:00 PM**, with a break for lunch between **1:00 PM and 3:00 PM**. It's important to note that the chapel can get busier during peak tourist seasons, so visiting early in the morning or later in the afternoon may offer a more peaceful experience.

Admission:
The entrance fee for the Brancacci Chapel is usually around **€6**, though this may change based on special events or exhibitions. There are often discounted prices for students and groups, so be sure to ask about any available deals.

Tips for Visiting the Brancacci Chapel
1. **Take Your Time**: Unlike some of the bigger museums in Florence, the Brancacci Chapel is relatively small, so it's easy to explore at a leisurely pace. Spend some time observing the intricate details of the frescoes. Don't rush—you'll appreciate the subtlety of the work more when you focus on one section at a time.
2. **Bring a Guidebook or Audioguide**: To truly understand the significance of the frescoes, consider getting a guidebook or renting an audioguide. The stories behind each fresco are fascinating and will enhance your experience of the chapel.

3. **Visit During Off-Peak Hours**: As mentioned, the chapel can get busy, especially in the summer. Try to visit early in the morning or later in the afternoon when the crowds tend to be smaller.
   4. **Combine with Nearby Attractions**: The **Brancacci Chapel** is located in the Oltrarno district, an area of Florence that's often overlooked by tourists. After your visit, take the time to explore the surrounding streets, filled with artisan workshops, quaint cafes, and the beautiful **Piazza Santo Spirito**.

Hidden Gardens and Quiet Courtyards

These tucked-away gems offer a chance to escape the crowds and immerse yourself in the calm beauty of the city's green spaces. Whether you're looking for a serene place to rest, a secluded spot for reflection, or simply a break from the bustling streets, Florence's gardens and courtyards provide the perfect respite. Here's a guide to some of the most enchanting spots that you may not find in every guidebook—but are well worth seeking out.

1. The Bardini Gardens
Address: Costa San Giorgio, 2, 50125 Firenze
Opening Hours: 8:15 AM - 7:00 PM (April to October); 8:15 AM - 5:00 PM (November to March)
Entrance Fee: €10 (adults), reduced for students and groups

The Bardini Gardens are one of Florence's most peaceful spots, offering sweeping views of the city and the Arno River. Tucked away on the hillside, it's a lesser-known alternative to the more famous Boboli Gardens. The garden's serene atmosphere, complete with terraced levels, fountains, and sculptures, invites visitors to wander through its lush greenery.

A personal recommendation: take the time to visit the upper terrace, where you can sit on one of the benches and enjoy a perfect view of the Ponte Vecchio and the city's rooftops. It's one of those places where you'll want to just sit back and breathe in the tranquility, all while admiring the strikingly beautiful landscape.

2. The Rose Garden (Giardino delle Rose)
Address: Viale Giuseppe Poggi, 2, 50125 Firenze
Opening Hours: 9:00 AM - 8:00 PM (April to September), 9:00 AM - 5:00 PM (October to March)
Entrance Fee: Free

Located just below the Piazzale Michelangelo, the Rose Garden offers a spectacular panoramic view of Florence, especially at sunset. While it's open to the public year-round, it's particularly stunning in spring when the roses are in full bloom. The garden, with over 350 varieties of roses, provides a fragrant escape from the city's busy streets.

A real hidden treasure in the garden is the small Japanese area with its unique bonsai trees. It's perfect for a quiet stroll or even a moment of reflection as you sit on one of the stone benches surrounded by the scent of flowers and the distant hum of the city.

3. The Garden of San Miniato al Monte
Address: Via delle Porte Sante, 34, 50125 Firenze
Opening Hours: 8:00 AM - 6:00 PM daily
Entrance Fee: Free

San Miniato al Monte is one of Florence's most iconic churches, but it's the serene garden behind it that is often overlooked by tourists. This tranquil spot, perched high above the city, offers spectacular views and a peaceful atmosphere. The garden's layout is simple, but its calm beauty provides a perfect place to sit and unwind.

From here, you can also take in a magnificent view of Florence below, with the terracotta roofs, the Ponte Vecchio, and the Duomo all laid out before you. The church is a peaceful retreat, and if you happen to visit during a time when the church bells ring, it adds a wonderful soundtrack to the peaceful garden setting.

4. The Garden of the Innocents (Giardino degli Innocenti)
Address: Piazza della Santissima Annunziata, 50122 Firenze
Opening Hours: 8:00 AM - 7:00 PM daily
Entrance Fee: Free

Situated in the historic heart of Florence, near the Piazza della Santissima Annunziata, this garden is often overlooked by many visitors. It's a quiet and beautifully landscaped space surrounded by the imposing, historical architecture of the Ospedale degli Innocenti. The garden's central fountain, shaded paths, and quiet corners provide a peaceful atmosphere perfect for a midday break.

Many visitors miss this garden simply because it's tucked behind the Ospedale's arcades, making it feel like a secret within the heart of the city. But it's a delightful escape—especially for those who enjoy taking a few moments to pause and reflect amid stunning greenery.

5. The Laurentian Library and Its Courtyard

Address: Piazza San Lorenzo, 6, 50123 Firenze
Opening Hours: 9:00 AM - 5:00 PM (closed on Mondays)
Entrance Fee: Free for library use; guided tours available at a cost

While not a traditional garden, the Laurentian Library's courtyard offers a peaceful, quiet respite from the busy streets of Florence. The courtyard is accessible to visitors of the library, and it is one of the more understated yet beautiful spots in the city. With its elegant columns and serene ambiance, it feels like stepping into a time capsule.

The library itself, designed by Michelangelo, is an architectural masterpiece. After a tour of the library, take some time to rest in the courtyard, where you'll often find local residents enjoying the quietude. It's a place that encourages reflection and is perfect for book lovers looking to escape the usual tourist crowds.

6. The Giardino delle Medici

Address: Viale delle Mille, 50100 Firenze
Opening Hours: 9:00 AM - 6:00 PM
Entrance Fee: Free

Although not as famous as the Boboli or Bardini Gardens, the Giardino delle Medici is a lovely little space that provides some respite for those who want to avoid the crowds. The garden is attached to the Medici villas and is surrounded by beautiful Renaissance-era architecture. Its serene pathways, shaded trees, and peaceful fountains make it an ideal spot to relax, read, or enjoy a snack.

Why You Should Visit These Hidden Gardens
Florence is a city that's constantly bustling with activity. Whether you're admiring the masterpieces at the Uffizi or exploring the streets around Piazza del Duomo, it's easy to get swept up in the crowds. But these hidden gardens and courtyards offer a quiet retreat.

Not only do they allow you to slow down, but they also provide a different perspective of Florence. You'll see the city through the eyes of locals who know where to find peace amid the urban hustle. It's in these lesser-known spaces that you can truly feel the magic of Florence—its timeless beauty and hidden corners that reveal themselves only to those who seek them out.

Practical Tips:
- Wear comfortable shoes, as many gardens are located on hills or have uneven paths.
- Take some water and perhaps a snack with you, especially if you plan to relax in these spaces for a while.
- Visit early in the morning or later in the afternoon for the most peaceful experience and to avoid the heat of midday.

Artisan Workshops and Vintage Boutiques

Florence is a city renowned for its artistry, and beyond its famous museums and churches, you'll find a vibrant world of artisans keeping centuries-old traditions alive. Whether you're strolling through the narrow streets of the Oltrarno district or browsing the boutiques tucked away in historic buildings, Florence's artisan workshops and vintage boutiques offer something special for those who want to take home a piece of the city's rich craft heritage.

The Craftsmanship Legacy of Florence
Florence has been a center of art and craftsmanship for centuries, and the city continues to thrive as a hub for skilled artisans. In the past, Florence

was home to the Medici family, who were famous patrons of the arts and helped establish the city as a center of Renaissance culture. Today, the same attention to detail, precision, and love for craftsmanship is evident in the workshops of local artisans, many of whom still use age-old techniques passed down through generations.

Leather Workshops

One of Florence's most celebrated artisan products is leather. The city has a long history of leatherworking, dating back to the 13th century, and it's still one of the best places in the world to buy handmade leather goods. The **San Lorenzo Market**, located near the Basilica of San Lorenzo, is one of the best spots to explore leather products, but if you want a more personal experience, visiting a workshop is the way to go.

A must-visit is **Scuola del Cuoio**, located behind the Basilica di Santa Croce at **Via San Giuseppe, 5r**. This workshop, which was founded in 1950, offers a fascinating glimpse into the world of traditional leatherworking. The artisans here still use methods that have been passed down for centuries. You can watch them create custom leather bags, wallets, and belts using nothing but their hands and specialized tools. The best part? You can take part in a workshop yourself and create your own leather item to take home!

Why visit? It's a great opportunity to learn about Florence's leather history and pick up a high-quality, handmade piece of craftsmanship that will last a lifetime.

Handmade Jewelry

Florence is also home to some of the finest goldsmiths in the world, particularly around the **Ponte Vecchio**. As you walk across this iconic bridge, you'll notice the small shops selling beautifully crafted jewelry. These boutiques often feature intricate designs, such as the famous Florentine "filigree" work, which involves delicate, lace-like patterns made from gold and silver.

If you're looking for a truly unique piece, visit **Roberto Coin**, at **Via della Condotta, 12r**. Known for his exquisite jewelry that blends traditional Italian craftsmanship with modern designs, Roberto Coin's boutique showcases pieces that reflect the artistry Florence is known for. Each piece is made with care and attention to detail, and the boutique offers personalized services, allowing you to have a one-of-a-kind item created just for you.

Why visit? Florence's jewelry-making tradition is centuries-old, and buying a piece from a local artisan is not only an investment in beauty but also in history.

Vintage Boutiques:

Florence is also a treasure trove for vintage lovers. Whether you're searching for unique clothing, accessories, or home decor, the city's vintage boutiques are brimming with one-of-a-kind items. Unlike mass-produced fashion, vintage shops offer a more personal experience—many of the items have their own stories to tell, and you can often trace their history back to a specific time or place.

One of the best places to start is **Cavalli e Nastri**, a chic vintage store at **Via della Spada, 14r**. This boutique is known for its selection of high-quality vintage clothing, including designer pieces from the 20th century. You'll find everything from 1950s cocktail dresses to 1980s Chanel handbags. It's a great spot to pick up something truly unique that will set you apart.

Why visit? Vintage shopping in Florence is about more than just finding a great deal. It's an opportunity to own a piece of history and support local businesses while doing so.

Florentine Ceramics:

Another form of Florentine craftsmanship worth exploring is ceramics. Florence is known for its beautiful hand-painted pottery, and many of the artisans still work in traditional workshops where you can watch the entire process—from shaping the clay to painting intricate designs by hand.

A particularly charming place to visit is **Bottega dei Cerchi**, at **Piazza San Giovanni, 3r**. This workshop and store specialize in beautifully painted plates, vases, and bowls, all showcasing the vibrant colors and intricate patterns that are characteristic of Florentine ceramics. You can even watch the artisans at work and learn about the techniques used to create each piece.

Why visit? If you're looking for a unique souvenir that showcases Florence's artistic heritage, a piece of handmade ceramic pottery is a perfect choice.

Practical Tips for Shopping in Artisan Workshops and Boutiques
- **Bring Cash:** Many smaller artisan workshops in Florence only accept cash, so it's a good idea to carry some on hand.
- **Don't Be Afraid to Ask Questions:** The artisans love to share their craft and often offer a personal demonstration of their process. It's a great way to learn about the art and the people behind it.
- **Look for Authenticity:** To ensure you're buying an authentic handmade product, ask about the materials and the techniques used. Local artisans are proud to share the history behind their creations.
- **Opening Hours:** Many artisan workshops in Florence are closed on Sundays and may close for lunch in the afternoon, so it's best to plan your visit accordingly. Check online or call ahead to avoid disappointment.

Day Trips to Medieval Villages Nearby

These villages are perfect for day trips, allowing you to step away from the bustle of the city and experience a more tranquil, traditional side of Italy. Whether you're drawn to the rolling hills, ancient stone buildings, or the idea of getting lost in narrow cobblestone streets, these nearby towns are well worth the journey. Here are a few of the most captivating medieval villages you should consider visiting during your stay in Florence.

1. San Gimignano: The City of Towers

Located about 1 hour from Florence by car, San Gimignano is one of Tuscany's most famous medieval villages. Known for its impressive skyline, the town is often referred to as the "City of Towers" because it was once home to 72 towering structures, built by wealthy families during the 12th and 13th centuries. Today, 14 of these towers still stand, giving the town its unique and picturesque profile.

Why You Should Visit:

San Gimignano is like stepping into a medieval fairytale. As you wander through its narrow streets, you'll pass by well-preserved buildings and gorgeous squares. Don't miss a visit to the Collegiate Church of Santa Maria Assunta, which boasts stunning frescoes. For those who enjoy wine, the town is also famous for its white wine, Vernaccia di San Gimignano. You can tour the local wineries, taste their wines, and purchase a bottle to bring back home.

Address and Practical Tips:
- San Gimignano, 53037 Tuscany
- The town is easily accessible by car (about 1 hour) or by bus from Florence.
- The main attractions, including the towers and churches, are open year-round, but visiting in the early morning or late afternoon helps avoid the busiest crowds.

2. Volterra: Etruscan and Medieval Charm

About an hour and a half from Florence, Volterra is a stunning town perched atop a hill with breathtaking views of the surrounding Tuscan countryside. What makes Volterra unique is its rich history that dates back to the Etruscan period, around 700 BC. You'll find remnants of this ancient civilization, along with medieval architecture, making it an ideal place to explore both Etruscan and medieval history.

Why You Should Visit:
Volterra is quieter than its more famous neighbors, making it an excellent escape for those seeking peace and beauty. The town is known for its alabaster, a soft stone that has been used in crafting decorative objects for centuries. You can visit local artisans' shops where they still carve this stone into intricate sculptures and jewelry. Volterra is also home to the Roman Theater and the Etruscan Museum, which houses fascinating ancient artifacts. A stroll through the town reveals lovely medieval piazzas and stone buildings, such as the Palazzo dei Priori.

Address and Practical Tips:
- Volterra, 56048 Tuscany
- If traveling by car, it's a beautiful 1.5-hour drive from Florence.
- The town is also accessible by bus. Once there, be sure to walk up to the Etruscan Gate and enjoy the panoramic views of the rolling hills.

3. Certaldo: A Hidden Gem
Certaldo, located about 40 minutes from Florence, is often overlooked by tourists, which makes it an even more rewarding destination. This medieval town is split into two parts: the modern Certaldo Basso and the hilltop Certaldo Alto, which is where the main attractions lie. The medieval town was once home to the famous writer Giovanni Boccaccio, author of "The Decameron," and you can visit his house while in town.

Why You Should Visit:
What makes Certaldo so special is its authentic feel. The town is not flooded with tourists, so you can wander through its cobbled streets and explore its ancient churches, medieval palaces, and small family-owned shops in peace. You can also take a funicular ride up to Certaldo Alto, offering spectacular views of the surrounding landscape. Make sure to stop by the Church of San Jacopo for its peaceful ambiance and beautiful frescoes.

Address and Practical Tips:
- Certaldo, 50052 Tuscany
- It's a quick 40-minute drive or train ride from Florence, making it one of the most accessible day trips.
- Take the funicular from Certaldo Basso to the top for the best views and a leisurely exploration of the medieval town.

4. Greve in Chianti: Tuscany's Wine Heartland

For those who want to combine history with a glass of local wine, a trip to Greve in Chianti is a must. Situated about 30 minutes from Florence, this charming town sits at the heart of the Chianti wine region. Surrounded by vineyards and olive groves, Greve is known for its wine, as well as its scenic beauty and relaxed atmosphere.

Why You Should Visit:
Greve in Chianti offers a perfect balance of medieval charm and natural beauty. Stroll through the town's main square, Piazza Matteotti, where you'll find a variety of wine shops and local food markets. You can also visit the Wine Museum to learn about the region's centuries-old wine-making tradition. If you're a wine lover, you'll want to book a wine-tasting tour at one of the local wineries, where you can sample some of the best Chianti wines while taking in the stunning vineyard views.

Address and Practical Tips:
- Greve in Chianti, 50022 Tuscany
- Easily reached by car (around 30 minutes) or public transport from Florence.
- Plan to visit a winery for a tour and tasting – many offer lunch and a chance to enjoy the surroundings.

5. Radda in Chianti: A Peaceful Village Amidst Vineyards

A little further into the Chianti region, Radda in Chianti is another delightful medieval village that offers a quieter, more intimate experience than some of the larger towns. Set in the hills, the village is surrounded by vineyards and offers spectacular views of the surrounding countryside.

Why You Should Visit:
Radda is known for its medieval charm, cobbled streets, and stone buildings. You can visit the Church of San Niccolò, stroll around the town's lovely square, and enjoy its traditional Tuscan atmosphere. The village also makes a great base for exploring the surrounding vineyards and olive groves, and there are several family-owned wineries that offer tours and tastings.

Address and Practical Tips:
- Radda in Chianti, 53017 Tuscany
- About 1.5 hours from Florence by car.
- The town is accessible by public bus, but having a car gives you the freedom to explore the nearby vineyards and olive groves.

Local Tips for Exploring the Unknown Florence

Beyond the well-trodden tourist paths, there are hidden corners waiting to be discovered. Whether you're an art enthusiast, a foodie, or someone looking for peace away from the crowds, there's a secret side to Florence that's just as captivating. Let's dive into some local tips for exploring the Florence most tourists miss, but the Florentines know and love.

1. Wander Through the Oltrarno District

While the city's historic center is a must-see, crossing the Arno River to the Oltrarno district opens a whole new world. This charming neighborhood is often overlooked by tourists, yet it's where the real Florentine life happens. With its cobblestone streets, artisan workshops, and vibrant atmosphere, it's a perfect place for those who want to experience the soul of Florence.

Why Visit?
The Oltrarno is home to Florence's craftsmen—leatherworkers, goldsmiths,

and woodworkers who still practice their trades as they have for centuries. You'll find quaint shops where you can watch artisans at work, creating everything from hand-stitched leather bags to intricate jewelry. It's also a great spot for a quiet coffee or a glass of wine at one of the charming local cafés.

Real-Life Example:
One of my favorite spots is the **Bottega del Cinquecento** (Via Santo Spirito, 6r), a small workshop where you can find beautiful hand-carved wooden frames, just like the ones used in the Uffizi Gallery. Chatting with the owner, an elderly artisan named Giovanni, is a treat. He'll share stories of the city's history as you watch him craft each frame by hand.

2. Discover the Hidden Gardens: The Bardini Gardens

Florence is famous for the Boboli Gardens, but just a short walk away, you'll find the less crowded **Bardini Gardens** (Costa San Giorgio, 2). While the Boboli Gardens attract many visitors, Bardini feels like a secret garden, tucked away behind the hillside. Here, you'll find peaceful spaces, blooming flowers, and a fantastic view of the city.

Why Visit?
Bardini Gardens offer tranquility away from the hustle and bustle of Florence's main squares. The gardens have a variety of landscapes—vistas overlooking the city, fountains, and a beautiful wisteria-covered pergola. If you're lucky, you might even catch a local Florentine artist sketching the scenery.

Practical Tip:
Admission is around €10, and it's less crowded early in the morning. If you can, plan to visit right when it opens for a serene, almost private experience. The view of the city from the top terrace is worth the price of admission.

3. A Quiet Moment at the Rose Garden

For a more intimate experience, head to **Giardino delle Rose** (Viale Giuseppe Poggi, 2). This small, often-overlooked garden is located at the foot of Piazzale Michelangelo and is a perfect spot for some downtime.

Why Visit?
This garden has over 350 varieties of roses and offers a peaceful retreat with panoramic views of the city. It's a great place to unwind after a day of sightseeing or enjoy a quiet moment with a book. There's even a lovely statue dedicated to the poet **Alfred Lord Tennyson**, adding a touch of literary charm to the area.

Personal Anecdote:
I stumbled upon this garden one late afternoon when I was exploring the area near Piazzale Michelangelo. I had been walking for hours and needed a break. The roses were in full bloom, and the scent in the air was intoxicating. It was the kind of moment that made me fall in love with Florence all over again—a quiet, peaceful escape from the usual tourist crowds.

4. The Sant'Ambrogio Market for Local Flavors

While the **Mercato Centrale** (San Lorenzo Market) is famous for its vibrant food stalls, **Sant'Ambrogio Market** (Piazza Ghiberti) is where locals do their shopping. This open-air market is a great spot to experience the authentic Florentine way of life, away from the crowds.

Why Visit?
You can find fresh produce, meats, cheeses, and local products like Tuscan olive oil and truffle-infused treats. It's a wonderful place to pick up ingredients for a picnic or chat with the vendors. They're happy to offer samples of their products, and you might even be invited to taste a homemade slice of *focaccia* from a local bakery.

Practical Tip:
Visit on a weekday morning for a more relaxed experience. If you're a foodie, this is an ideal place to pick up a few things for a picnic in one of Florence's beautiful parks or gardens.

5. Exploring the Artisans' Workshops

Florence has a rich history of craftsmanship that is still alive and well today. Hidden in the corners of the city are workshops where you can observe artisans creating everything from bespoke leather goods to intricate gold jewelry.

Why Visit?
A visit to a Florentine artisan workshop offers you a rare opportunity to see centuries-old techniques in action. Whether it's a leather-making workshop in **San Frediano** or a small goldsmith's shop along the **Ponte Vecchio**, watching the artisans at work brings you closer to the city's cultural roots.

Personal Tip:
If you're looking for a unique souvenir, I recommend heading to **Scuola del Cuoio** (Via San Giuseppe, 5r), a historic leather school inside the Santa Croce Monastery. It's not just a shop; you can watch leather artisans work and even buy high-quality items directly from the workshop.

6. Stroll Through the Streets of San Niccolò

The **San Niccolò** district, located just below Piazzale Michelangelo, is often skipped by visitors, but it's one of Florence's most charming neighborhoods. It's full of narrow streets lined with trattorias, bars, and independent shops.

Why Visit?
This area has a bohemian vibe, with art galleries, quaint cafes, and small boutiques offering unique, handcrafted goods. It's an ideal place to wander aimlessly, enjoy a leisurely lunch, and soak in the atmosphere of authentic Florence.

Real-Life Example:
One afternoon, I found a hidden little café called **Caffè degli Artigiani** (Via di San Niccolò, 58), which had the best *cappuccino* I've ever tasted. Sitting outside, I watched the locals pass by, and for a moment, I felt like I was part of the city's daily rhythm.

Art and Culture

The Renaissance Revolution:

Florence is, without a doubt, the birthplace of the Renaissance—an era that sparked a dramatic shift in art, science, and culture. Walking through the city, you're essentially stepping into the heart of this revolutionary period. From the moment you set foot in Florence, it's clear that the Renaissance didn't just influence art—it *is* art here. Let's take a journey through Florence's incredible art legacy, explore why the city's treasures are still so relevant, and why you absolutely should visit the places that define this cultural rebirth.

A Brief Overview of the Renaissance in Florence

The Renaissance began in Florence in the 14th century, during a time when Europe was transitioning from the medieval to the modern world. The term itself means "rebirth," and Florence was at the forefront of this intellectual and artistic revival. This period marked the rediscovery of ancient Greek and Roman knowledge, the development of perspective in painting, and a surge of humanism that placed man at the center of the universe.
Florence's wealth and political stability under the Medici family were crucial in fostering this movement. The Medici were not just powerful rulers; they were passionate patrons of the arts, funding the works of artists who would go on to shape the course of history.

Florence's Art Revolutionaries

Some of the most famous artists of the Renaissance were either born in or spent significant time in Florence. Michelangelo, Leonardo da Vinci, Donatello, Sandro Botticelli, and Raphael all contributed to this transformative period, and their works remain on display in Florence today. Take **Michelangelo**, for example. One of his earliest masterpieces, the *David*, is housed in the **Galleria dell'Accademia** (Via Ricasoli, 58/60), and standing in front of it is an awe-inspiring experience. The statue isn't just a representation of the biblical hero; it embodies the Renaissance ideals of human perfection and strength.

Then there's **Botticelli**, whose *The Birth of Venus* graces the walls of the **Uffizi Gallery** (Piazzale degli Uffizi, 6). This painting isn't just an iconic work of art—it's a symbol of Florence's embrace of beauty, mythology, and idealized human form. Seeing these masterpieces in person, rather than in a book or online, gives you a deeper understanding of the era's revolutionary impact.

Key Renaissance Art Stops in Florence
1. **Uffizi Gallery**
   Address: Piazzale degli Uffizi, 6
   Date: Open daily, closed Mondays
   Activities: Explore over 2,000 works of art, including pieces by Botticelli, Titian, Raphael, and Caravaggio.
   Why You Should Visit: The Uffizi is one of the most important art museums in the world, housing an extensive collection of Renaissance masterpieces. Every gallery feels like stepping through time, as you witness the evolution of art during the Renaissance. It's where Florence's art history truly comes alive.
2. **Galleria dell'Accademia**
   Address: Via Ricasoli, 58/60
   Date: Open daily, closed Mondays
   Activities: See Michelangelo's *David*, along with other sculptures and works of art from the Renaissance period.
   Why You Should Visit: *David* is undoubtedly the star attraction here, but the entire museum offers a fascinating look at Renaissance sculpture and art. The gallery offers a quiet, contemplative environment to appreciate the work that revolutionized the art world.
3. **Palazzo Vecchio**
   Address: Piazza della Signoria, 1
   Date: Open daily, closed Mondays
   Activities: Visit the palace where the Medici family ruled and explore frescoes by artists like Giorgio Vasari.
   Why You Should Visit: The **Palazzo Vecchio** is an incredible mix of art,

history, and architecture. The Medici apartments, painted with frescoes that highlight their wealth and influence, give visitors a sense of what it was like during the Renaissance. The palace itself was the center of political and cultural life in Florence during the Renaissance.

4. **Basilica di Santa Croce**
   Address: Piazza Santa Croce, 16
   Date: Open daily
   Activities: Visit the tombs of Florence's most famous Renaissance figures, including Michelangelo, Galileo, and Machiavelli.
   Why You Should Visit: Santa Croce is not just a beautiful church but also the resting place of some of the most important figures in art, science, and literature. The frescoes and architecture alone are worth the visit, but the historical significance of the tombs makes it an essential stop for anyone interested in the Renaissance.

Personal Anecdote:
On my first visit to Florence, I was struck by how *alive* the art felt. It wasn't just hanging on walls in a sterile museum—each piece seemed to speak to me, telling stories of creativity, rebellion, and exploration. I'll never forget standing in front of *David* in the Galleria dell'Accademia. It wasn't just the grandeur of the statue that captivated me, but the way it seemed to embody the spirit of Florence itself: bold, innovative, and full of hope for the future.

Similarly, at the Uffizi, I remember walking through the galleries with a sense of discovery, each room opening up new possibilities in art, from Botticelli's *Venus* to Da Vinci's early works. The Renaissance wasn't just about the past—it was about creating a vision for the future, and that vision is still present in every corner of Florence.

Why Florence's Art Legacy Still Matters Today
Florence's Renaissance legacy continues to influence not just art but the world as we know it. The ideals of humanism, the focus on the individual, and the exploration of new artistic techniques changed the course of history. Walking through Florence today, you're walking through a living

museum, where every corner reveals a story of innovation, beauty, and the pursuit of knowledge.

Whether you're an art lover or just someone who appreciates history, Florence's Renaissance art will leave a lasting impression. This city is not just a place to visit—it's a place to experience, to live in, and to be inspired by.

Artisanal Crafts:

Florence isn't just a city of iconic art and stunning architecture; it's also a hub for artisanal craftsmanship that has been passed down through generations. If you're looking for a truly authentic souvenir or want to immerse yourself in the traditions of Italian craftsmanship, Florence offers plenty of opportunities to discover some of the finest leatherworking, goldsmithing, and other artisanal crafts.

Leatherworking:

Florence is world-famous for its leather, and for good reason. The city's leather-making tradition dates back to the Middle Ages, and today it remains one of the city's most cherished crafts. The most famous area to explore Florence's leather craft is the **San Lorenzo Market**, a vibrant marketplace that's home to countless leather shops. These small family-owned stores create everything from handbags to jackets to belts, each piece showcasing the high quality and detail for which Florence is known.

One standout is **Scuola del Cuoio** (Leather School), located in the **Basilica di Santa Croce**. Not only can you buy beautifully handcrafted leather goods here, but you can also watch skilled artisans at work. Visitors can take workshops where they learn the basics of leathercraft, or simply marvel at the craftsmanship displayed in the school's gallery. The address is **Via San Giuseppe 5r**, and it's a must-visit for anyone interested in hands-on crafting. The school offers workshops, typically by appointment, where you can create your own leather item.

Real-life example: I recently visited **Scuola del Cuoio** during my trip and had the chance to observe a master artisan working on a custom leather bag. It was an incredible experience to see the painstaking care that went into every stitch. Afterward, I treated myself to a gorgeous handmade wallet that I know will last for decades. It's this quality that makes Florence's leather so revered worldwide.

Goldsmithing:

Florence is also renowned for its goldsmithing tradition, particularly the craftsmanship found along the **Ponte Vecchio**. For centuries, this bridge has been home to jewelers and goldsmiths, creating exquisite pieces of jewelry that reflect the city's rich artistic history. The shops along the bridge are family-run businesses, and many of them specialize in crafting jewelry using techniques that have been passed down for generations.

The most famous goldsmiths are found in **Ferruccio Santini** (Ponte Vecchio, **Via Ponte Vecchio 17r**), a business that's been operating since 1911. Visitors can stop by and witness artisans handcrafting intricate pieces using traditional tools, with gold and silver being worked into pieces of unparalleled beauty. Whether you're looking for an elegant ring, a statement necklace, or an heirloom-quality bracelet, the jewelers of Florence are the place to find something truly unique.

Real-life anecdote: During my visit, I had the pleasure of speaking with a third-generation jeweler who worked in one of these Ponte Vecchio shops. He told me how his grandfather taught him the art of creating detailed, delicate filigree work, which involves twisting gold wires into beautiful patterns. He showed me a custom ring he had just finished, and the attention to detail was extraordinary. I ended up purchasing a pair of earrings that have become one of my most treasured keepsakes from Florence.

Other Florentine Crafts:

Florence isn't just about leather and gold. The city is home to numerous other artisanal crafts that reflect its rich artistic heritage. One such craft is **paper marbling**, a centuries-old technique that involves floating pigments on water and then transferring them onto paper, creating unique, swirling patterns. Many shops in Florence sell these beautiful marbled paper goods, from journals to stationery, perfect for anyone who wants a piece of authentic Florence.

A great place to explore this craft is the **Officina Profumo-Farmaceutica di Santa Maria Novella**, located at **Via della Scala 16**. While primarily known for its fragrant products, the store also showcases stunning marbled paper goods that make for a lovely and thoughtful souvenir.

Another craft you shouldn't miss is **ceramics**. Florence has a long history of producing fine ceramics, and there are many places to find beautifully painted pottery and vases. One such place is **La Ceramica Artistica** at **Via Sant'Agostino 1r**, where you can watch artisans hand-paint designs and create custom pottery. The craftsmanship here is incredible, and it's a great spot to pick up a unique, handcrafted piece of Florence.

Why You Should Visit Florentine Craft Studios

Florence's artisanal studios offer a chance to experience the city in a completely unique way. The pieces made here are not just souvenirs; they are works of art, each carrying the story of the artisan who created it. Whether you choose to bring home a leather handbag, a custom-made piece of jewelry, or a beautifully marbled journal, you're taking a piece of Florence's creative heritage with you.

For those who want a deeper connection with the crafts, many of these artisans offer workshops where you can try your hand at creating something yourself. These experiences can range from leatherworking to ceramics, and they're an incredible way to spend an afternoon in Florence.

Practical Tips for Shopping for Artisanal Goods
1. **Ask About the Craft**: Don't be afraid to ask artisans about their process and the history behind their work. Many are happy to share stories about how their craft has evolved through the years.
2. **Watch for Custom Work**: If you're looking for something truly special, many shops offer custom orders. Whether it's a personalized piece of jewelry or a custom leather wallet, this is a great way to ensure you have something unique.
3. **Expect to Pay for Quality**: These are handcrafted items, so the prices can reflect the time and skill involved. However, the quality you're getting is unmatched.

Opera and Classical Music Venues

If you're a lover of music, particularly the opera, you're in for a treat. From grand theaters with centuries of tradition to smaller, intimate venues that showcase the best of local talent, Florence offers a variety of ways to experience the beauty of classical music.

Teatro del Maggio Musicale Fiorentino

Address: **Piazzale Vittorio Gui, 1, 50144 Firenze**
Website: www.maggiofiorentino.com

The **Teatro del Maggio Musicale Fiorentino** is Florence's premier opera house and one of Italy's most renowned cultural institutions. Founded in 1933, the theater is home to the famous **Maggio Musicale Fiorentino** festival, an annual celebration of classical music, opera, and ballet that takes place every spring. The festival attracts top international performers and composers and is a must-see for any classical music enthusiast visiting Florence.

The theater itself is an architectural marvel, with stunning acoustics and a grand interior that enhances the musical experience. Whether you're attending a performance as part of the festival or catching a year-round opera, you'll be treated to an unforgettable evening of world-class performances. The theater regularly stages works by composers like Verdi, Puccini, and Mozart, along with more contemporary works, ensuring there's something for everyone.

Why You Should Visit:
The Maggio Musicale festival is a cultural cornerstone of Florence, making it a unique experience for those lucky enough to visit during its run. Even outside of the festival, the performances held here are top-tier. It's an unmissable spot for anyone who appreciates opera and classical music.

Teatro della Pergola

Address: **Via della Pergola, 18, 50121 Firenze**
Website: www.teatrodellapergola.com

If you're looking for a venue with a little more historical charm, the **Teatro della Pergola** is Florence's oldest theater, dating back to 1656. This beautifully preserved Baroque-style theater has hosted legendary performances by Italian composers and musicians for centuries. Today, it still serves as an important venue for opera, classical concerts, and theater productions.

The theater's intimate size means that no matter where you sit, you'll feel up close to the performers, enhancing the overall experience. It's a more traditional venue compared to the modern Teatro del Maggio, with gilded details and plush seating that reflect Florence's rich cultural heritage.

Why You Should Visit:
The Teatro della Pergola offers an atmosphere of classical grandeur that you can't find in modern venues. Whether you're attending an opera, ballet, or symphony performance, the beauty of the space and the passion of the performers will leave you in awe. The venue is also a great place to experience the historic side of Florence's musical legacy.

Santa Croce Church and Its Musical Offerings

Address: **Piazza di Santa Croce, 16, 50122 Firenze**
Website: www.santacroceopera.it

For a more unconventional experience, **Santa Croce Church** offers a series of classical concerts and operatic performances in one of Florence's most famous churches. Known for its stunning frescoes and the tombs of great Italians like Galileo and Michelangelo, Santa Croce's acoustics are equally impressive, making it an extraordinary venue for live music.

Throughout the year, the church hosts a range of classical music events, from intimate chamber concerts to full-scale operas. The combination of historic setting, beautiful acoustics, and world-class performances makes this a truly special place to experience classical music.

Why You Should Visit:
Attending a concert at Santa Croce is an unforgettable experience. Not only do you get to enjoy top-tier music, but you also have the opportunity to do so in a place of immense historical significance. It's a rare blend of music, art, and history that you won't find elsewhere.

Real-Life Experience:

One of my most cherished memories in Florence was attending an opera at the **Teatro del Maggio Musicale Fiorentino**. I was fortunate enough to see a performance of **La Traviata**, and it was an evening to remember. The grandeur of the theater, the beauty of the opera, and the sense of history that surrounded me made for a magical experience. The stunning acoustics in the theater made every note feel alive, and I could feel the emotion of the performers in every aria.

What struck me most was the audience's level of appreciation. Florence, with its deep ties to the arts, attracts music lovers from all over the world, and being surrounded by people who truly understood the nuances of the opera made the experience even more enriching. It's the kind of place where you leave feeling inspired, grateful, and connected to a long tradition of musical excellence.

Practical Tips for Opera Lovers in Florence
1. **Buy Tickets in Advance:** Florence's top opera venues can sell out quickly, especially during the Maggio Musicale festival. It's best to purchase your tickets well in advance.
2. **Dress the Part:** While there's no strict dress code, many people like to dress up for the occasion. A smart-casual outfit is often perfect, but if you're attending a special performance, you may want to go for something more formal.
3. **Check the Schedule:** Opera seasons can vary, and not all performances are in Italian. Make sure to check the schedule for any translated performances or English-language subtitled operas.
4. **Arrive Early:** Arriving early will give you time to appreciate the venue and take in the atmosphere. Plus, it allows you to find your seat and settle in before the music begins.

Notable Museums Beyond the Classics

Florence is a city brimming with artistic masterpieces and historical treasures, many of which can be found in its world-famous museums like the Uffizi Gallery and the Galleria dell'Accademia. But for those willing to venture off the well-worn path, Florence offers several lesser-known museums that are just as rich in culture and charm. These museums give a unique insight into the city's past and its continuing role in the world of art, science, and design. If you're someone who wants to explore beyond the classics, here are some must-visit spots.

Museo Stibbert: A Glimpse into Florence's Eccentric History
Address: Via Stibbert 26, 50134 Florence
Hours: Tuesday to Sunday, 10:00 AM - 6:00 PM (Closed on Mondays)
Ticket Price: €10 (Reduced for students and groups)

Tucked away in the residential area of Florence, the Museo Stibbert is a hidden gem that is often overlooked by mainstream tourists. The museum is the private collection of Frederick Stibbert, an Englishman who spent much of his life in Florence collecting an extraordinary array of armor, weapons, and historical artifacts from around the world. The Stibbert Museum stands out for its eccentric and vast collection of over 50,000 items, including knightly armor, samurai swords, and even Egyptian relics.

Walking through the museum feels like stepping into a time machine. You can see full suits of armor displayed in dramatic poses, as if frozen mid-battle. My personal favorite? The Japanese armor collection—meticulously crafted and steeped in centuries of tradition. The museum's vast collection offers not just an aesthetic experience, but also a fascinating look at the history of warfare across cultures. If you're into history, armor, or just quirky, off-the-beaten-path attractions, this is a must-see.

Museo Galileo: Science Meets Art
Address: Piazza dei Giudici 1, 50122 Florence
Hours: Daily, 9:30 AM - 6:00 PM
Ticket Price: €10

Florence's intellectual history is just as impressive as its artistic legacy, and the Museo Galileo offers a fascinating window into the world of Renaissance science. Named after the famous Florentine scientist Galileo Galilei, the museum is home to an impressive collection of scientific instruments that made history. It's a place where science and art converge, showcasing beautiful devices used in astronomy, navigation, and medicine from the 16th and 17th centuries.

The museum's centerpiece is the original telescopes used by Galileo, including the one he used to make his revolutionary discoveries about the stars and planets. It's mind-blowing to think that these simple yet precise instruments changed the way we see the universe. If you're a science enthusiast or simply curious about how Florence helped shape the scientific world, this museum is a must-visit. Don't miss the interactive exhibits, which allow you to step into Galileo's shoes and explore the scientific innovations of the time.

Museo del Bargello:
Address: Via del Proconsolo 4, 50122 Florence
Hours: Monday to Sunday, 8:15 AM - 1:50 PM
Ticket Price: €12

The Museo del Bargello is one of Florence's most underrated museums, and yet it's home to some of the most iconic sculptures from the Renaissance period. The museum itself is housed in a former barracks and prison, and its collection focuses primarily on sculptures and decorative arts. The museum showcases works by Michelangelo, Donatello, and Verrocchio, including Donatello's *David*, one of the earliest representations of the biblical hero in the nude.

I'll never forget my first visit to the Bargello—standing face-to-face with these masterful sculptures feels like being in the presence of history itself. The museum's intimate setting lets you get up close to the pieces, something that is sometimes difficult to do at larger, more crowded museums. It's an absolute gem for art lovers looking for a deeper, more personal experience with Florence's Renaissance artistry.

Museo di San Salvi:
Address: Via di San Salvi 16, 50135 Florence
Hours: Tuesday to Sunday, 10:00 AM - 6:00 PM (Closed on Mondays)
Ticket Price: Free entry

If you want to escape the hustle and bustle of the tourist crowds, the Museo di San Salvi is a perfect quiet retreat. Located inside a former convent and asylum, this museum houses an impressive collection of 19th-century Tuscan art. The focus here is on the paintings, drawings, and sculptures that reflect the socio-political changes in Tuscany during the 1800s.

What makes the Museo di San Salvi particularly special is its tranquil environment. You'll often find yourself alone with the artworks, creating a meditative experience that allows you to truly absorb the pieces. The museum also frequently hosts temporary exhibitions, making it a dynamic spot for contemporary art lovers. It's a great stop for anyone looking to explore the often-overlooked art scene in Florence.

Museo della Moda e del Costume:
Address: Palazzo Pitti, Piazza de' Pitti 1, 50125 Florence
Hours: Tuesday to Sunday, 8:15 AM - 6:50 PM
Ticket Price: €10 (Part of the Pitti Palace ticket)
Florence has long been a center for fashion, and the Museo della Moda e del Costume inside the Pitti Palace is a celebration of that history. The museum showcases a collection of costumes, textiles, and accessories dating back to the 18th century, offering a fascinating look at how fashion has evolved over time.

The museum's highlight is its collection of clothing worn by the Italian aristocracy, from intricate gowns to tailored suits. For anyone with an interest in fashion history or design, this museum offers a unique glimpse into the style and luxury of Florence's elite. It's also worth noting that the museum occasionally hosts temporary exhibitions, bringing in collections from the fashion world's top designers.

Why You Should Visit These Museums
Florence is a city that has been at the heart of the world's artistic and intellectual movements for centuries. While the Uffizi and the Accademia often steal the spotlight, these lesser-known museums offer a more intimate experience that highlights the diverse and ever-evolving culture of Florence. Each of these museums provides a unique perspective—whether it's the world of science, history, or fashion—and allows you to see the city from a different angle.

Incorporating these museums into your itinerary allows you to dive deeper into Florence's soul, making your visit all the more enriching and memorable. Plus, you'll have the chance to explore parts of the city that are often missed by the typical tourist, adding a layer of authenticity to your journey.

Street Art and Contemporary Exhibits

From the colorful murals on forgotten walls to cutting-edge installations in galleries, the city's modern art scene is thriving, offering a fresh and exciting perspective on the city's culture. If you're an art lover or simply someone who enjoys seeing cities evolve through creative expression, Florence's street art and contemporary exhibits should not be missed.

Street Art: Where to Find It

Unlike many cities that have embraced street art on a grand scale, Florence's street art scene is somewhat more hidden, creating an exciting treasure hunt for art enthusiasts. The city's historic center may be dominated by medieval buildings and grand palaces, but venture into neighborhoods like **San Frediano**, **Oltrarno**, and **Santo Spirito**, and you'll start to discover vibrant murals, graffiti, and urban art installations that have become part of the city's modern cultural fabric.

One of the most notable examples is the work of **C215**, a French artist whose stencil portraits of various figures (including Florence's own historical characters) adorn several walls around the city. His pieces, often emotionally evocative, blend the old with the new, adding an unexpected twist to Florence's art scene. In the **Oltrarno district**, you'll find large-scale murals painted by both Italian and international street artists, transforming mundane alleyways and old buildings into colorful canvases.

Another place to explore is **Piazza Santa Maria Novella**, where smaller, yet striking pieces can be spotted. The area around **Via dei Serragli** is also home to some impressive street art, where vibrant colors pop against the stonework of traditional Florence buildings. These works often change as new artists take over, making the experience of discovering Florence's street art a dynamic one. Keep an eye out as you wander—every turn might reveal something new.

Why You Should Visit

Florence's street art scene may seem out of place at first glance, but it provides a vital contrast to the city's classical reputation. For those who are familiar with the city's historic treasures, the juxtaposition of old and new offers a refreshing view of Florence. These urban pieces engage with the city's history in surprising ways, making you reconsider how contemporary creativity fits into the old-world charm of Florence.

For example, the **Urban Jungle Project**, a collaborative initiative by various street artists, uses nature-inspired murals to comment on environmentalism and conservation. It's an art form that speaks not only to the city's aesthetic but also to pressing global issues. This project, located around the **Ponte alla Carraia** area, uses the walls as canvases to discuss the relationship between urbanization and nature.

Beyond the murals and spray-painting, street art in Florence often addresses social and political themes. Artists in the city have used their work to make statements about everything from immigration to gender equality, often drawing from Florence's rich artistic heritage and weaving in modern sensibilities.

Contemporary Art Exhibits and Galleries
Florence's contemporary art galleries are pushing boundaries, making the city an exciting destination for those interested in the cutting edge of art. While traditional museums like the Uffizi and Accademia hold timeless masterpieces, you don't have to look far to find contemporary pieces that offer new perspectives on modern life.
A must-visit is the **Museo Novecento**, located in the heart of Florence's historic center, which is entirely dedicated to 20th and 21st-century Italian art. The museum often showcases works that are more experimental and innovative than what you might expect from Florence's traditional art scene. The exhibits here range from abstract paintings to sculptures and

multimedia installations, with an emphasis on exploring Italy's complex political and social history through art.

Another notable venue is **Firenze Off**, a contemporary art space that aims to promote alternative forms of visual expression. Located near the **Santa Croce district**, the gallery showcases works from international artists, often in unconventional spaces like old warehouses or public parks. It's a great place to discover new, avant-garde art in a non-traditional setting.

Florence also hosts the **Biennale Internazionale dell'Arte Contemporanea** (International Biennale of Contemporary Art), an event that takes place every two years. The biennale brings together artists from all over the world to display their work in various locations across the city. From large-scale installations to more intimate, experimental works, the event showcases how contemporary art can be integrated into the fabric of Florence.

Personal Experience and Tips for Art Lovers

I once stumbled upon a small art installation while wandering through **Via dei Sassetti**, an alley off the main tourist routes. What looked like an unassuming set of abandoned buildings turned out to be home to a pop-up art exhibit that explored the theme of digital decay. The exhibit featured interactive pieces and even virtual reality elements. It was a fascinating contrast to the more traditional museums I had seen earlier in the day.

If you're looking for something a bit more interactive, check out **Firenze Art Week**. This event gathers a variety of contemporary artists, local and international, to showcase their works in various galleries and open spaces. During my visit last year, I had the chance to meet several artists, see live demonstrations, and even take part in workshops. It was an unforgettable experience that deepened my connection to Florence's thriving contemporary art scene.

For a more personalized experience, I recommend booking a street art tour. These guided tours will take you through lesser-known neighborhoods, providing insights into the artists' backgrounds and the stories behind each piece. Plus, you'll have the chance to learn about Florence's transition from a Renaissance city to one embracing modernity.

Seasonal Festivals and Cultural Events

Florence isn't just a city of timeless art and stunning architecture—it's also a vibrant hub of cultural festivities that celebrate everything from its rich Renaissance history to modern creative expressions. Whether you're visiting during the warm summer months or the crisp fall, there's always something happening in this dynamic city. Here's a closer look at some of Florence's most exciting seasonal festivals and cultural events that make this city come alive with energy and tradition.

1. The Florence Carnival (February/March)

Although Venice often steals the spotlight with its grand Carnival celebrations, Florence's Carnival offers its own unique flair. This event, typically held in February or March, marks the beginning of Lent and is filled with colorful parades, masquerade balls, and street performances. The highlight is the *"La Rificolona"*, a traditional lantern festival that takes place on the night of September 7, where children and families walk through the streets carrying lanterns and singing folk songs.

Address: Various locations across the city.
Why You Should Visit: The Carnival provides a great opportunity to see the locals embrace their traditions. It's a fun, lively event perfect for families or anyone looking for an authentic Italian experience. Plus, the vibrant lantern processions at night are simply magical.

2. Scoppio del Carro (Explosion of the Cart) - Easter Sunday

One of the most unique and thrilling events in Florence is the *Scoppio del Carro*, or "Explosion of the Cart," which takes place every Easter Sunday. The festival has ancient origins, dating back to the 12th century, and it centers around a cart (decorated with intricate designs) filled with fireworks. The excitement begins when a priest lights a rocket, called the "*colombina*", that travels down a wire to the cart, triggering a stunning firework display. If everything goes as planned, it is said that Florence will have a prosperous year ahead.

Address: Piazza del Duomo
Date: Easter Sunday (date varies each year)
Activities: Watch the colorful parade with historical reenactments, followed by the fireworks.
Why You Should Visit: The spectacle of fireworks lighting up the sky against the backdrop of Florence's stunning cathedral is unforgettable. It's also a fantastic way to immerse yourself in centuries-old Florentine traditions.

3. Festa della Madonna della Neve (Feast of Our Lady of the Snow) - August 5

This is a particularly beloved event for the people of Florence, especially in the Oltrarno district. The festival celebrates the legend of the Madonna who appeared to a wealthy Roman family and instructed them to build a church in her honor. On the Feast Day, the streets of the Oltrarno come alive with processions, music, and a parade of locals dressed in traditional costumes. In the evening, a fireworks display takes place, marking the culmination of the day's celebrations.

Address: Piazza Santo Spirito, Oltrarno
Date: August 5
Activities: Processions, music performances, and fireworks.
Why You Should Visit: The local atmosphere in the Oltrarno is always a joy to experience, and this festival offers a more intimate, traditional side of Florence that you might not find in the city's busier tourist spots. Plus, the fireworks light up the sky in a truly spectacular way.

4. Calcio Storico (Historic Florentine Football) – June 24

This event is not for the faint-hearted. *Calcio Storico* is an ancient and incredibly violent game, combining soccer, rugby, and wrestling. Played annually on June 24, the festival marks the feast day of Florence's patron saint, Saint John the Baptist. Teams representing the four historic districts of Florence (Santa Croce, San Giovanni, Santa Maria Novella, and Santo Spirito) compete in a game that involves tackling, punching, and scoring goals—often in a cloud of dust and chaos.

Address: Piazza Santa Croce
Date: June 24
Activities: Watch the intense and passionate matches, enjoy the local food and drink.
Why You Should Visit: This is one of the most thrilling and eccentric festivals in Florence. The atmosphere is electric, and the passion of the spectators is contagious. If you enjoy unique cultural events, this is a must-see!

5. Maggio Musicale Fiorentino (May)

If you're a fan of music, Florence's *Maggio Musicale Fiorentino* is the festival for you. Held throughout May, it's one of Italy's most prestigious classical music festivals. The event features a series of performances, including operas, symphonic concerts, ballet, and chamber music, all held in some of the most iconic venues in Florence. The festival is a great way to experience the city's rich artistic heritage and modern-day cultural vibrancy.

Address: Various venues including the Teatro Comunale, Teatro del Maggio
Date: Throughout May
Activities: Attend performances by world-class musicians, composers, and dancers.
Why You Should Visit: The *Maggio Musicale* offers an unparalleled

experience for music lovers. Whether you're attending a grand opera or an intimate chamber concert, you'll feel the city's love for music come to life.

6. Florence Summer Festival (June – July)

If you're visiting Florence in the summer, the Florence Summer Festival is a highlight you won't want to miss. This outdoor music festival takes place during June and July in the beautiful *Cortile del Bargello*, offering concerts ranging from pop and rock to classical music and jazz. With the warm Tuscan evenings and the charm of Florence's architecture, it's the perfect setting for an unforgettable musical experience.

Address: Various outdoor venues, including the *Cortile del Bargello*
Date: June – July
Activities: Attend live performances from internationally renowned artists.
Why You Should Visit: If you're a music lover, Florence Summer Festival is one of the best ways to experience Florence under the stars while enjoying great performances in a historical setting.

Florentine Cuisine and Dining Experiences

Classic Florentine Dishes to Try

Whether you're wandering through the historic center or tucked away in a cozy trattoria, Florence's food scene offers an array of dishes that are deeply rooted in the city's history. Here are seven classic Florentine dishes that you absolutely must try, each brimming with local flavor and cultural significance.

1. Bistecca alla Fiorentina (Florentine Steak)

Arguably the most iconic of Florentine dishes, **Bistecca alla Fiorentina** is a true celebration of Tuscan cuisine. This thick-cut, bone-in T-bone steak is traditionally grilled over wood or charcoal, seasoned simply with salt, pepper, and a drizzle of olive oil. The steak is served rare (with the inside a juicy, tender red), which may be a surprise for those who prefer their steak cooked through.

Where to try it:
One of the best places to enjoy this dish is at **Trattoria Mario** (Vicolo della Misericordia 1r), a beloved local spot where you can enjoy authentic, rustic Tuscan food in an unpretentious setting. For a more upscale experience, head to **La Giostra** (Borgo Pinti 12/r), known for its cozy ambiance and incredible steaks.

Price:
Expect to pay around €25-€35 for a generous portion.

2. Ribollita (Tuscan Vegetable Soup)

If you're in Florence during the colder months, you'll definitely want to try **Ribollita**, a hearty soup made from day-old bread, cannellini beans, and a medley of seasonal vegetables like cabbage, kale, and carrots. The word "ribollita" literally means "reboiled," as the soup was traditionally made with leftovers from the previous day's meal, making it both frugal and flavorful.

Where to try it:
One place where you can savor an excellent Ribollita is **Caffè Gilli** (Piazza della Repubblica 39r), which has been serving Tuscan dishes since 1733. It's a great spot to take a break from sightseeing and enjoy this filling, comforting dish.
Price:
Typically, Ribollita costs around €8-€12 for a bowl.

3. Lampredotto (Traditional Florentine Street Food)
If you're looking for an authentic street food experience in Florence, **Lampredotto** is a must-try. This sandwich, made from slow-cooked beef tripe (the fourth stomach of a cow), is served in a crusty roll with a splash of salsa verde (green sauce) or spicy chili sauce. It's an acquired taste, but for those who love trying new things, it's a deliciously local experience.
Where to try it:
For the best Lampredotto, head to the **Trippaio del Porcellino** (Mercato del Porcellino, Piazza del Mercato Nuovo), where the stall's friendly staff serve up piping hot sandwiches that locals swear by.
Price:
A lampredotto sandwich will cost around €5-€7, making it a great, affordable snack.

4. Pappardelle al Cinghiale (Wild Boar Pasta)
Wild boar has long been a fixture in Tuscan cuisine, and **Pappardelle al Cinghiale** (pasta with wild boar sauce) is a rich and satisfying dish. The wide, ribbon-like pappardelle pasta is coated in a slow-cooked sauce made from tender wild boar, tomatoes, and aromatic herbs. The sauce is deep, earthy, and full of flavor, perfect for pairing with a glass of Chianti wine.
Where to try it:
For an authentic take on this dish, visit **Osteria All'Antico Vinaio** (Via dei Neri 74r), a casual yet popular eatery known for its incredible Tuscan fare.
Price:
A serving of Pappardelle al Cinghiale usually costs around €12-€18.

5. Schiacciata alla Fiorentina (Florentine-Style Cake)
After all those savory dishes, you'll want something sweet to balance it out. **Schiacciata alla Fiorentina** is a traditional Florentine cake typically served during Carnival (pre-Lenten season) but can be found year-round. This spongy, slightly sweet cake is often topped with powdered sugar and decorated with the city's symbol, the Florentine lily.
Where to try it:
Pasticceria Nencioni (Via Maffia 4r) is a local favorite for this dessert. The bakery is small but renowned for its light, delicious Schiacciata.
Price:
Slices of Schiacciata alla Fiorentina typically cost around €2-€4.

6. Cantucci e Vin Santo (Almond Biscuits with Sweet Wine)
No visit to Florence is complete without trying **Cantucci e Vin Santo**—almond biscuits that are perfect for dipping into a glass of Vin Santo, a sweet dessert wine. These crunchy biscuits are slightly hardened and best enjoyed with a slow sip of the wine, making it a perfect way to end a meal.
Where to try it:
Many restaurants will serve this dish as a dessert course, but for a true Vin Santo experience, head to **Caffè Pasticceria Rivoire** (Piazza della Signoria 5r). Their version is perfect for those who want to sit back and relax while watching the world go by.
Price:
Cantucci with Vin Santo typically costs around €6-€8 for a portion.

7. Pappa al Pomodoro (Tomato and Bread Soup)
Another comforting Tuscan dish, **Pappa al Pomodoro** is a thick soup made with ripe tomatoes, basil, garlic, and stale bread. While simple, the ingredients come together beautifully to create a flavorful, rustic dish that captures the essence of Tuscany's philosophy of using fresh, local produce.
Where to try it:
For a truly homey, traditional experience, visit **Trattoria Sostanza** (Via del Porcellana 25r). It's known for serving some of the best homemade Tuscan dishes in a charming, local setting.

Price:
Pappa al Pomodoro usually costs around €9-€12 for a hearty portion.

Where to Find the Best Trattorias and Osterias

If you're craving the essence of Tuscan cuisine, then stepping into these humble yet warm spaces will make you feel like you're dining in a local's home. Let's explore some of the best spots in Florence where you can enjoy hearty meals and a true taste of Tuscany.

1. Trattoria Sostanza
- **Address:** Via del Porcellana, 25/r, 50123 Florence
- **Price:** Main courses range from €10 to €20
- **Specialties:** Butter chicken, artichoke omelet
- **Why It's Special:** If you want to experience a Florentine classic, Sostanza should be on your list. Established in 1869, this trattoria serves up mouth-watering traditional dishes. The butter chicken here is legendary — the meat is so tender, it practically melts in your mouth. Don't skip the artichoke omelet either, especially during the artichoke season. It's simple, rustic, and absolutely delicious.

I remember the first time I visited, I sat in the cozy, no-frills dining room surrounded by locals. The atmosphere was warm and inviting, and the servers greeted everyone like family. That's the beauty of trattorias in Florence: they're as much about the food as they are about the sense of belonging.

2. Osteria Vini e Vecchi Sapori
- **Address:** Via dei Magazzini, 1/r, 50122 Florence
- **Price:** Around €15-€25 per person
- **Specialties:** Ribollita, pappa al pomodoro
- **Why It's Special:** Tucked away near the Ponte Vecchio, this cozy osteria feels like an undiscovered gem. The menu at Vini e Vecchi

Sapori is full of heartwarming Tuscan comfort food, with ribollita (a rich vegetable and bread soup) and pappa al pomodoro (tomato and bread soup) being two of their best-loved dishes. These are perfect for a chilly day in Florence and provide a taste of traditional Tuscan hospitality.

The best part? The owners are incredibly friendly and passionate about their food. I was lucky enough to strike up a conversation with the owner, who shared that the ribollita recipe was passed down from his grandmother. There's nothing like enjoying food with a story behind it.

3. Trattoria da Burde
- **Address:** Via Pistoiese, 6, 50145 Florence
- **Price:** Main courses from €12 to €20
- **Specialties:** Bistecca alla Fiorentina, ribollita
- **Why It's Special:** For many Florentines, Trattoria da Burde is the place to go for a perfect bistecca alla Fiorentina (Florentine steak). This family-run institution serves up some of the best steak in the city, cooked over a wood fire to perfection. If you're a steak lover, this is a must-visit spot.

I had the pleasure of dining here with a group of friends during my last trip, and it was an experience we'll never forget. The atmosphere is both lively and intimate, with large groups of locals often gathered to enjoy their meals together. The bistecca was perfectly charred on the outside and juicy on the inside — truly a taste of Florence.

4. Osteria di Passignano
- **Address:** Località Passignano, 3, 50028 Tavarnelle Val di Pesa, Florence
- **Price:** €25-€40 per person
- **Specialties:** Truffle pasta, Tuscan meats
- **Why It's Special:** While technically just outside Florence, Osteria di Passignano is worth the short drive for its extraordinary food and stunning setting. Located in the heart of the Chianti wine region, the osteria specializes in dishes made with locally sourced ingredients, from truffle pasta to exquisite Tuscan meats. Pair

your meal with a glass of Chianti Classico — a truly authentic Tuscan experience.

I'll never forget the breathtaking view from the terrace, overlooking vineyards and rolling hills. Dining here felt like stepping into a storybook, and the food was just as magical. If you're a fan of the flavors of Tuscany, this is a place you shouldn't miss.

5. Trattoria Mario

- **Address:** Via Rosina, 2r, 50123 Florence
- **Price:** €10-€18 per dish
- **Specialties:** Florentine steak, pappa al pomodoro
- **Why It's Special:** Located near the San Lorenzo market, Trattoria Mario is a popular spot among locals and tourists alike. It's a bustling, no-frills eatery that serves hearty, flavorful meals at very reasonable prices. The bistecca alla Fiorentina is a standout, along with their signature pappa al pomodoro. The place is small, often packed, and has a family-style atmosphere.

I first stumbled upon Trattoria Mario when I was wandering through the San Lorenzo area. It was so packed that we had to wait for a table, but it was definitely worth the wait. The food arrived quickly, hot, and fresh, and the vibe inside was so lively that it truly felt like a local's hangout. The best part? The prices are incredibly affordable for the quality you get.

6. La Trattoria da Tito

- **Address:** Via San Gallo, 112/r, 50129 Florence
- **Price:** €20-€30 per person
- **Specialties:** Florentine steak, veal stew
- **Why It's Special:** La Trattoria da Tito is a traditional spot that's beloved by locals. They've been serving up hearty, well-prepared Tuscan classics for decades. The veal stew here is a standout, along with their tender, perfectly grilled bistecca alla Fiorentina. What I love most about this trattoria is how the chefs take pride in the quality and presentation of every dish.

When I visited, I sat at a rustic wooden table and enjoyed the rich flavors of a slow-cooked veal stew paired with a local Chianti. It was the kind of meal that made me feel like I was part of the family — that's the charm of these Florentine trattorias.

7. Trattoria Il Contadino
- **Address:** Via del Palazzo Bruciato, 7, 50122 Florence
- **Price:** €12-€20 per dish
- **Specialties:** Wild boar ragù, pappardelle pasta
- **Why It's Special:** Situated near the Santa Croce district, Trattoria Il Contadino is a charming place known for its wild boar ragù and hand-rolled pappardelle pasta. This place offers a real taste of the Tuscan countryside in the heart of Florence, with rustic, flavorful dishes that showcase the region's rich food traditions.

Street Food in Florence:

When you think of street food in Florence, the image of an old, crusty sandwich filled with tender meat, topped with a green sauce, and served hot is probably the first thing that comes to mind. This humble yet beloved dish is none other than **Lampredotto**, a staple of Florentine street food culture. But lampredotto is just the beginning—Florence offers an array of street foods that cater to all tastes, from savory snacks to sweet treats.

Lampredotto:
Let's start with the most iconic street food in Florence—**Lampredotto**. Made from the fourth stomach of a cow, lampredotto is slow-cooked in a broth with herbs and spices, and served on a soft, crusty roll. It's usually topped with a green sauce made of parsley, garlic, and vinegar. Although it might sound unusual to the uninitiated, it's one of the most delicious, tender, and flavorful things you can eat in Florence.

You'll find lampredotto being served at food carts, especially around markets like **Mercato di San Lorenzo** and **Piazza della Stazione**. The sandwich is typically served with your choice of sauce, and you can opt for a second round of broth to dip the sandwich in, giving it a juiciness that is irresistible.

Where to try Lampredotto:
- **Trippaio del Porcellino**: Located near **Piazza del Mercato Nuovo** (just by the famous **Porcellino** statue), this stall serves a fantastic lampredotto, always fresh and tender.
    - Price: Around €5 for a sandwich.
- **Lampredotto da Nello**: A well-loved spot near **Piazza della Stazione**, where locals and tourists alike line up for a bite of this authentic street food.
    - Price: €4-€5 per sandwich.

Panino con la Mortadella:
Though lampredotto steals the spotlight, the **Panino con la Mortadella** is another popular street snack you shouldn't miss. Mortadella, an Italian sausage with a subtle, mellow flavor and a smooth texture, is often sliced thin and served in a sandwich. In Florence, you'll often find this classic street food served in a simple but tasty roll.

This is the perfect snack to grab when you're strolling through the streets of Florence—whether you're in a rush or just taking a break from sightseeing. The flavors are straightforward, but the quality of the mortadella and the freshness of the bread are what make it so special.

Where to try Mortadella Sandwich:
- **All' Antico Vinaio**: Famous for its sandwiches, this spot near **Piazza del Duomo** offers an excellent version of the mortadella sandwich.
    - Price: €3-€4.

Frittura di Pesce:
If you're a fan of seafood, **Frittura di Pesce** is a must-try street food. This mix of fresh, fried seafood includes shrimp, squid, and small fish, all lightly battered and fried to golden perfection. It's served in a paper cone, making it easy to walk around while enjoying it. Frittura di Pesce is perfect for those who want to savor the flavors of the Mediterranean while exploring Florence's streets.

The taste is fresh and crispy, with the salty goodness of seafood balanced perfectly by a squeeze of lemon.
Where to try Frittura di Pesce:
- **Trattoria Sostanza**: Located in the **Santa Maria Novella** area, this eatery is known for its classic Tuscan fried fish. Though it's a sit-down restaurant, the street food vibe is very much alive.
    - *Price*: Around €8-€10 for a serving.

Schiacciata:
No trip to Florence is complete without trying **Schiacciata**, a type of flatbread that is often served as a street snack. This bread is crispy on the outside but soft and airy on the inside. It's commonly stuffed with a variety of fillings such as prosciutto, salami, or even cheese and olives.
If you want a quick bite before heading to the galleries or museums, Schiacciata is the perfect snack. It's light, yet satisfying, and it allows you to enjoy the flavors of Tuscany in every bite.
Where to try Schiacciata:
- **Forno Pugi**: Located in **Piazza della Repubblica**, this bakery is famous for its fresh schiacciata. Whether you choose it plain or stuffed, it's always a delicious treat.
    - *Price*: €2-€5 depending on the filling.

Piadina:
Though Piadina originates from the Emilia-Romagna region, it's a favorite among Florentine street food enthusiasts. This thin, flatbread is folded over and filled with a variety of ingredients, including meats, cheeses, and vegetables. Piadina is often served warm and is perfect for a quick lunch or a light snack. It's very similar to a quesadilla or wrap, but with a distinctively Italian twist.
Where to try Piadina:
- **La Piadineria**: Close to **Piazza San Giovanni**, you'll find this stand that serves freshly made piadine with a variety of fillings.
    - *Price*: €4-€6 per piadina.

Cecina:
If you're in the mood for something savory but gluten-free, try **Cecina**, a crispy chickpea pancake that's a beloved snack in Tuscany. It's simple—just chickpea flour, olive oil, water, and a pinch of salt—but the result is a crispy, golden snack that's perfect on its own or served as a filling between slices of bread. Often topped with fresh rosemary, cecina offers a satisfying combination of crunch and flavor.

Where to try Cecina:
- **I' Girone De' Ghiotti**: This place near **Piazza della Signoria** serves a variety of traditional Tuscan street foods, and their cecina is one of the best you'll find.
  - *Price*: €3-€5.

Gelato:
Finally, no visit to Florence is complete without indulging in some **gelato**. While gelato is everywhere in Italy, Florence is home to some of the best gelaterias. Whether you prefer classic flavors like pistachio and chocolate or more adventurous ones like pear and ricotta, you'll find the perfect scoop.

Enjoy your gelato while wandering the streets of Florence—maybe along the **Ponte Vecchio** or near **Piazza del Duomo**—and savor a sweet moment in this beautiful city.

Where to try Gelato:
- **Gelateria dei Neri**: Located near **Piazza Santa Croce**, this gelateria is known for its rich, creamy gelato made with fresh ingredients.
  - *Price*: €3-€5 for a cone or cup.

Wine Tasting:

This iconic region, nestled between Florence and Siena, is known for its picturesque vineyards, charming villages, and, of course, its world-renowned Chianti Classico wines. If you're a wine lover—or even if you're just looking to add a bit of local flavor to your trip—this is an experience you won't want to miss. Here's everything you need to know about the Chianti wine-tasting experience.

What is Chianti Wine?
Chianti wine, specifically Chianti Classico, is made primarily from the Sangiovese grape, offering a delicious balance of rich fruit flavors and earthy notes. It's the quintessential Tuscan red wine, with a distinctive taste that reflects the region's unique terroir. Chianti Classico is often labeled with a black rooster seal (Gallo Nero), which signifies it has come from the heart of the Chianti region. Whether you're sipping a smooth, fruity Chianti or one with more complex tannins, it's impossible not to be captivated by the flavors.

Where to Taste Chianti Wines
Wine-tasting experiences in Chianti aren't just about sipping wine—they're about immersing yourself in the landscape, history, and passion that make these wines so special. Here are seven incredible spots where you can enjoy the best of Chianti:

1. **Castello di Verrazzano (Greve in Chianti)**
    - **Address:** Località Verrazzano, 5, 50022 Greve in Chianti FI, Italy
    - **Price:** Starting at €25 for a basic tour and wine tasting
    - **What's Special:** This historic winery, housed in a 16th-century castle, offers one of the most scenic wine-tasting experiences. The views of the surrounding vineyards are spectacular, and the wines are rich with history. During the tour, you'll get a chance to learn about the castle's origins and how wine has been produced here for centuries.
    - **Where to Buy It:** You can buy their wines directly from the winery or online.

2. **Castello di Brolio (Gaiole in Chianti)**
    - **Address:** 53013 Gaiole in Chianti SI, Italy
    - **Price:** From €35 per person for a guided tour and wine tasting

- **What's Special:** Castello di Brolio is a must-visit for anyone who wants a taste of Chianti's aristocratic heritage. Owned by the Ricasoli family, who have been making wine here for over 500 years, the estate offers a mix of history and great wine. Their Chianti Classico is a standout, with a strong focus on Sangiovese.
- **Where to Buy It:** Available at the winery or through their online store.

3. **Fattoria La Vialla (Rignano sull'Arno)**
   - **Address:** Via di Meleto, 76, 50067 Rignano sull'Arno FI, Italy
   - **Price:** Around €30 for a guided tour and tasting of four wines
   - **What's Special:** Fattoria La Vialla is an organic farm that produces wines, olive oil, and other Tuscan specialties. The wine tasting here offers an intimate look at sustainable farming and production methods. Their Chianti Classico is a real crowd-pleaser, and you'll also get a chance to taste their other organic products.
   - **Where to Buy It:** You can purchase their products directly at the farm or online.

4. **Podere Il Palazzino (Radda in Chianti)**
   - **Address:** Via Casole, 2, 53017 Radda in Chianti SI, Italy
   - **Price:** From €40 per person for a guided tasting
   - **What's Special:** Located in the heart of Chianti Classico, Podere Il Palazzino offers a family-friendly wine experience. The estate produces elegant and full-bodied wines, and visitors can enjoy a walk through the vineyards, learning about the farming techniques that make this area so unique.
   - **Where to Buy It:** The winery has an online store where you can purchase their wines.

5. **Il Molino di Grace (Greve in Chianti)**
   - **Address:** Via Molino di Grace, 10, 50022 Greve in Chianti FI, Italy

- **Price:** Starting at €25 for a basic tour and tasting
- **What's Special:** A boutique winery with a focus on high-quality, small-batch Chianti Classico. Their vineyards are situated at a high altitude, which contributes to the unique flavor profile of their wines. The staff is friendly and knowledgeable, and the tasting experience is relaxed but informative.
- **Where to Buy It:** You can purchase their wines at the winery or online.

6. **Ruffino (Pontassieve)**
   - **Address:** Via San Michele a Pontenuovo, 50, 50065 Pontassieve FI, Italy
   - **Price:** Starting at €20 for a guided wine-tasting tour
   - **What's Special:** A household name in Italian wines, Ruffino offers a wide range of Chianti wines. Their vineyards are beautiful and the tasting experience includes a tour of their cellars, which date back to the 1800s. The wines are refined, and you'll taste some of the best the Chianti region has to offer.
   - **Where to Buy It:** Ruffino wines are available for purchase at the winery, in Italian stores, or online.

7. **Tenuta di Nozzole (Greve in Chianti)**
   - **Address:** Località Nozzole, 50022 Greve in Chianti FI, Italy
   - **Price:** From €30 for a guided tour and tasting
   - **What's Special:** This stunning estate is set in the heart of the Chianti Classico zone. With a perfect blend of tradition and modernity, Tenuta di Nozzole produces wines that are a true reflection of the land. Their Chianti is full-bodied and complex, and the tasting experience is tailored to each visitor's preferences.
   - **Where to Buy It:** You can purchase their wines directly from the estate or online.

Tips for Your Chianti Wine-Tasting Adventure
- **Book in Advance:** Many wineries, especially those that are small or family-owned, require reservations, particularly during peak tourist season.
- **Wear Comfortable Shoes:** Wine estates often require walking through vineyards or cellars, so comfortable footwear is a must.
- **Don't Rush the Tasting:** Wine tasting is about savoring the experience. Take your time to really appreciate the flavors, and ask the staff questions about the production process.
- **Take a Guided Tour:** Many wineries offer a guided tour, which can really enhance the experience, as you'll learn about the history and the process of making Chianti wine.
- **Take Home a Bottle:** There's nothing like enjoying a bottle of Chianti at home to remind you of your trip. Many estates offer shipping to your home country, or you can simply purchase a bottle to bring back with you.

Cooking Classes and Culinary Tours

The city's culinary scene is a blend of centuries-old tradition and fresh, locally sourced ingredients, making it the perfect place for a food adventure. Whether you're an amateur cook or a seasoned chef, there's a cooking class or culinary tour that will leave your taste buds dancing. Let's take a closer look at some of the best options in Florence for learning how to create authentic Tuscan dishes and experiencing the region's rich culinary heritage.

1. Culinary Institute of Tuscany – Cooking Classes
- **Location**: Via San Zanobi 60, 50129 Florence
- **Price**: Around €90–€150 per class
- **What's Included**: 3-4-hour classes focused on Tuscan cooking
- **Details**: The Culinary Institute of Tuscany offers hands-on cooking classes where you can learn to prepare traditional Tuscan dishes like fresh pasta, risotto, and classic desserts such as tiramisu. These classes are taught by local chefs who share their personal

cooking secrets. A typical class starts with a visit to a local market to pick out fresh ingredients, followed by a demonstration of various recipes. You'll prepare the dishes yourself, with plenty of time to savor the meal at the end.
- **Why It's Special**: The institute is known for its authentic, non-touristy approach, and the instructors are passionate about passing down their culinary knowledge.

2. Tuscan Cooking Class with a Local Chef
- **Location**: Private chef visits to your accommodation or a central venue
- **Price**: Around €80–€120 per person
- **What's Included**: In-home classes or group classes with a local chef
- **Details**: If you prefer an intimate, more personalized experience, booking a local chef to teach you in your own kitchen or at a central venue is an excellent option. Many Florentine chefs, such as those offering classes through platforms like **Eatwith**, will guide you through traditional recipes while you enjoy a glass of Tuscan wine. This type of class focuses on dishes you can easily recreate at home, like homemade pasta or braised meats, and the chefs often give you insights into family recipes passed down through generations.
- **Why It's Special**: The personal interaction with the chef allows you to ask questions and really immerse yourself in the local cooking techniques.

3. Walks of Italy – Florence Food Tour and Cooking Class
- **Location**: Piazza della Repubblica, Florence
- **Price**: €125–€160 per person
- **What's Included**: 3-hour guided food tour followed by a cooking class
- **Details**: Walks of Italy combines a food tour with a cooking class for a full Florence foodie experience. Start by exploring the San Lorenzo Market, one of the oldest food markets in the city, where

you'll sample cheeses, cured meats, and fresh produce. Afterward, you'll head to a local kitchen to cook a Tuscan meal, which might include dishes like pappa al pomodoro (tomato bread soup) or bistecca alla Fiorentina (Florentine steak). This tour is an excellent way to learn both about the ingredients and the preparation methods.
- **Why It's Special**: The combination of market exploration and cooking makes this tour unique. Plus, the small group size ensures plenty of one-on-one attention.

4. Cucina Lorenzo de' Medici
- **Location**: Via Ghibellina 87, 50122 Florence
- **Price**: From €70 per person
- **What's Included**: Hands-on cooking classes with a focus on Italian and Tuscan cuisine
- **Details**: Lorenzo de' Medici offers one of Florence's most famous cooking schools, with a variety of classes to choose from, including vegetarian cooking, pasta-making, and pizza workshops. Classes are interactive and taught by professional chefs, and you'll learn everything from how to make fresh pasta dough to crafting delicious sauces and preparing traditional desserts. Once you've prepared the meal, you can sit down and enjoy it with your fellow classmates, often paired with local wines.
- **Why It's Special**: The school is part of a renowned culinary institute, and the classes are taught in a state-of-the-art kitchen, giving you a truly professional cooking experience.

5. Tuscany by Bike – Culinary Cycling Tour
- **Location**: Departs from the center of Florence
- **Price**: €135 per person
- **What's Included**: Bicycle tour of the Tuscan countryside with a cooking class
- **Details**: For something a bit different, why not combine cycling with cooking? Tuscany by Bike offers a culinary cycling tour where you'll ride through the scenic hills surrounding Florence, stopping

at vineyards, olive groves, and local farms. Along the way, you'll stop to sample fresh produce and olive oil, before finishing the day with a cooking class where you'll learn how to prepare traditional Tuscan dishes using the ingredients you've just picked up. It's a great way to experience the rural side of Tuscany while learning to cook like a local.
- **Why It's Special**: This is perfect for active travelers who want to enjoy the outdoors while indulging in Florence's culinary delights.

6. Florence Cookery Class at In Tavola
- **Location**: Via Sant'Antonino 12, 50123 Florence
- **Price**: From €85 per person
- **What's Included**: 3-hour cooking class focused on Tuscan cuisine
- **Details**: In Tavola offers an excellent hands-on cooking experience where you'll prepare traditional Tuscan recipes using fresh, local ingredients. The class is led by a passionate local chef, and you'll make everything from pasta to dessert. At the end of the class, you'll enjoy the meal you've prepared, often accompanied by wine. It's a relaxed, fun environment that's perfect for both beginner and experienced cooks.
- **Why It's Special**: In Tavola's intimate setting allows for personalized instruction, making it ideal for small groups or families.

7. Gastronomic Florence – Street Food Tour
- **Location**: Via dei Neri, Florence (Meeting point)
- **Price**: Around €70 per person
- **What's Included**: 3-hour walking food tour, tasting local street foods
- **Details**: If you're not ready to cook just yet but still want to dive into the food scene, this street food tour is an excellent option. Take a stroll through Florence's backstreets with a local guide and sample some of the best street food in the city, including sandwiches, pastries, and sweet treats like gelato. You'll learn about the history and origins of each dish while enjoying bites

from local vendors. Afterward, you can consider signing up for a cooking class based on what you've tasted!
- **Why It's Special**: It's a fun, relaxed way to explore Florence through its food, with a knowledgeable guide to give you insider tips.

Markets and Local Food Producers

These markets are not only places to shop—they're also an opportunity to interact with locals, savor unique flavors, and discover authentic ingredients for your next culinary adventure.

1. Mercato Centrale (Central Market)
Address: Piazza del Mercato Centrale, 50136 Florence
Located in the San Lorenzo district, Mercato Centrale is one of Florence's most famous food markets. Split into two floors, the ground floor offers a bustling array of fresh meats, cheeses, fish, fruits, and vegetables. But what makes this market stand out is the second floor—a vibrant food court where local chefs serve up everything from fresh pasta to truffle-based dishes.
On any given day, you can see locals shopping for their weekly groceries while tourists savoring plates of pasta al tartufo (truffle pasta) or sipping local Chianti wines. Don't miss out on the stand that offers fresh, artisanal focaccia and pizza, perfect for a quick bite while you explore. The atmosphere here is lively, and it's an excellent spot to pick up fresh ingredients for a Tuscan meal.
Price: Expect to pay around €8-15 for a meal at the food court. Fresh produce and meats vary in price but generally start around €5 per kilo for vegetables.

2. Mercato di Sant'Ambrogio (St. Ambrogio Market)
Address: Piazza Ghiberti, 50122 Florence
A more off-the-beaten-path market compared to Mercato Centrale, Mercato di Sant'Ambrogio is where the locals shop. This market has a quieter, more traditional feel and offers everything from fresh fruit and vegetables to

high-quality meats and cheeses. You'll also find local vendors selling artisanal products like honey, preserves, and olive oil.

One of my favorite things to do at this market is to grab a seat at one of the nearby cafés after shopping and watch the world go by. You'll see vendors negotiating with regulars, creating a genuine, authentic vibe that you won't find in more tourist-heavy areas.

Price: Fresh local cheeses like pecorino can be bought for around €10-15 per kilo. Meat and fish prices vary but tend to be reasonable, especially for high-quality local products.

3. Mercato delle Pulci (Flea Market)

Address: Piazza dei Ciompi, 50122 Florence

While the Mercato delle Pulci is primarily a flea market, it's also a treasure trove of unique, locally-produced food items. You'll find stalls selling everything from Tuscan olive oils and local wines to artisanal balsamic vinegar and handmade pasta.

One memorable visit to this market led me to a tiny stall selling bottles of local wildflower honey. The vendor, a friendly Tuscan woman, offered me a taste of several varieties, each with a distinct flavor. It was a perfect example of how Florentine markets provide a hands-on, personalized shopping experience.

Price: You can expect to pay around €5 for a small jar of local honey or jams. Balsamic vinegar can range from €10 to €50, depending on the quality and age.

4. Farmers' Markets Around Florence

Florence has several smaller farmers' markets that pop up in various neighborhoods throughout the week, offering everything from organic vegetables to homemade pasta. These markets are great for anyone interested in farm-to-table dining and sustainable food.

One of the best known is the **Mercato Agricolo di Firenze** which sets up shop on Saturdays at **Piazza Santo Spirito**. Here, you'll find fresh, organic vegetables, fruits, meats, and dairy products directly from local farms. Many of the stalls also sell artisanal breads, jams, and cheeses.

Price: Organic produce here is usually priced slightly higher than supermarket goods, but it's well worth the quality. Expect to pay around €5-8 for a bag of fresh veggies.

5. Via dei Neri: Food Street Market
Address: Via dei Neri, 50122 Florence
Although not a traditional market, Via dei Neri is one of Florence's top streets for food lovers. Lined with food shops and small grocery stores, you'll find everything from truffle oils to homemade pasta. One shop that stands out is **La Prosciutteria**, where you can buy high-quality prosciutto and cheeses, paired with freshly baked bread. Many of the shops here allow you to sample products before buying, which is a fantastic way to discover the best of Tuscany's flavors.
Price: A sandwich with cured meats and cheeses at La Prosciutteria will cost you around €7-10, while a jar of truffle oil will set you back around €15-25.

6. The Tuscan Wine Market
Address: Via delle Cantine, 50122 Florence
Located in the heart of Florence's historic center, the **Tuscan Wine Market** specializes in local wines from all over Tuscany, including Chianti, Brunello di Montalcino, and Vino Nobile di Montepulciano. The market also sells olive oil, vinegars, and Tuscan grappa (a type of pomace brandy). Whether you're a wine connoisseur or a casual enthusiast, this place offers an excellent opportunity to purchase high-quality local bottles to take home as souvenirs.
Price: Wine bottles start from €10-15 for a basic Chianti, but more prestigious bottles can cost upwards of €30-40. Small bottles of olive oil are usually around €8-15.

7. Officina Profumo-Farmaceutica di Santa Maria Novella
Address: Via della Scala, 16, 50123 Florence
Though not a typical food market, **Officina Profumo-Farmaceutica** is a historic pharmacy that has been in operation since the 13th century. It is an iconic spot for Tuscan herbal products, and they sell high-quality extracts

and oils that are often used in cooking. You can find fragrant herbs like lavender and rosemary, perfect for bringing home a piece of Florence's culinary and cultural heritage.

While not your traditional food market, it's an excellent place to pick up gifts for food lovers, such as herbal teas, flavored honeys, and aromatic oils.

Price: Prices range from €10 for small jars of herbal tea to €25 for artisanal herbal products.

Foodie Itineraries: A Day of Eating in Florence

A day spent eating your way through Florence will treat you to a variety of flavors, from classic Tuscan dishes to unique street food experiences. Let me guide you through a food-centric day that will leave you full, happy, and even more in love with this beautiful city.

Morning: Breakfast at a Florentine Bar

Start your day like a local by visiting one of Florence's bustling cafés, or "bars" as they're known in Italy. The Italian breakfast is usually light, but satisfying, with a focus on coffee and pastry. A typical Florentine breakfast might include a cappuccino and a freshly baked *cornetto* (Italian croissant), filled with everything from jam to chocolate.

Where to go:

Caffè Gilli (Via Roma, 1r) – A Florentine institution since 1733, this elegant café is perfect for grabbing a coffee and pastry while soaking in the historic atmosphere. They're famous for their traditional *cappuccino* and sweet *cornetto*, but don't miss their *torta della nonna* (grandmother's cake), a creamy ricotta tart topped with pine nuts.

Price: Around €5-€8 for coffee and pastry.

Late Morning: Strolling Through Mercato Centrale

After breakfast, head to the **Mercato Centrale** (Piazza del Mercato Centrale, 50123) in San Lorenzo. This vibrant food market is a paradise for any foodie. On the ground floor, you'll find a variety of fresh produce, meats, cheeses, and local specialties, while the top floor has a modern food court where you can sample everything from fresh pasta to truffle sandwiches.

What to try:

- **Lampredotto**: A quintessential Florentine street food made from the fourth stomach of a cow, boiled and served on a bun with green sauce and spicy salsa. You'll find *lampredotto* stands just outside the market.

- **Truffle Sandwiches**: Head to the *La Trattoria da Burde* stand for a decadent truffle-infused sandwich. It's rich, savory, and a taste of Tuscan luxury.

Price: Around €5-€10 for each snack.

Lunch: Classic Tuscan Cuisine

For lunch, it's time to dive into some traditional Tuscan dishes. One of the best ways to experience the flavors of Florence is to try a hearty dish at a local trattoria. Florence is known for its *bistecca alla fiorentina* (Florentine steak) and *ribollita* (a rustic vegetable soup).

Where to go:
Trattoria Mario (Vicolo delle Misericordia, 2r) – A beloved local eatery that serves authentic Tuscan comfort food. Try the *ribollita*, a thick, vegetable-based soup that's a perfect lunch in the cooler months. It's a meal that's humble yet full of deep, earthy flavors.

Price: Around €15-€20 for a main dish.

Afternoon Snack: Gelato and Florence's Sweet Tooth

No food tour in Florence is complete without indulging in some gelato. After a fulfilling lunch, take a leisurely stroll toward **Piazza della Signoria** and treat yourself to a gelato break. Florence is home to some of the best gelato makers in the world, and you'll find gelaterias serving creamy, delicious flavors that go beyond the usual chocolate and vanilla.

Where to go:
Gelateria dei Neri (Via dei Neri, 20/22r) – Known for its rich, natural flavors, this gelateria offers everything from pistachio to seasonal fruit sorbets. I personally recommend the *ricotta and fig* flavor—pure Florence in a cup.
Price: Around €3-€6 for a small cone or cup.

Dinner: An Elegant Evening Feast

For dinner, head to a classic *osteria* for a true Florentine feast. The city is known for its rustic yet flavorful cuisine, with an emphasis on local, fresh ingredients. A Tuscan dinner typically starts with an appetizer, followed by a pasta dish, and ends with a hearty meat course.

Where to go:
Osteria Santo Spirito (Piazza Santo Spirito, 16r) – Located in the charming Oltrarno district, this is the place to enjoy the full Florentine dinner experience. Start with *crostini toscani* (toasted bread with chicken liver pâté), followed by *pappardelle al cinghiale* (wild boar pasta). Finish with *tiramisu* for dessert.

Price: Around €30-€40 for a full meal with wine.

Late Night: Wine and Small Bites

Florence's vibrant nightlife also means you can enjoy a glass of wine and some small bites to end your day. The best way to wrap up a food-centric day is with a glass of Tuscan wine, accompanied by some local cheese or olives.

Where to go:
Enoteca Pitti Gola e Cantina (Via de' Guicciardini, 49r) – Located just a short walk from the Pitti Palace, this intimate wine bar offers a great selection of local wines paired with Tuscan cheeses and meats. Whether you're a wine connoisseur or just starting your wine journey, the staff here will guide you through their extensive list. Try their *bruschetta* with olive oil as a perfect snack to go with the wine.

Price: Around €8-€15 for wine and snacks.

Nightlife and Entertainment

Best Bars and Wine Spots

Florence isn't just the birthplace of the Renaissance—it's also a city where the art of socializing thrives in its vibrant bars, wine spots, and cozy cafés. Whether you're unwinding after a day of sightseeing or seeking a lively night out, there's something here for every taste. Here's a guide to the best bars and wine spots in Florence, from historic wine cellars to trendy cocktail lounges, all offering a mix of local charm, delicious drinks, and unforgettable atmospheres.

1. Enoteca Pitti Gola e Cantina
- **Address:** Via Romana, 39r, 50125 Florence
- **Price:** Glasses of wine from €6-€10, with wine tastings from €25.
- **Why You Should Visit:** Nestled near the Pitti Palace, this intimate enoteca is a wine lover's paradise. Enoteca Pitti Gola offers an impressive selection of Tuscan wines, handpicked by sommeliers who are eager to guide you through the rich flavors of the region. What makes this spot stand out is the knowledgeable staff and the cozy atmosphere—perfect for sipping wine and pairing it with a selection of local cheeses and cured meats.

A personal recommendation: If you're unsure where to start, try the "Super Tuscan" wines that Florence is known for. The sommelier may also offer you a private tasting of a few, giving you a deep dive into the local terroir.
- **Activities:** Wine tastings, food pairings
- **How to Get There:** Take bus 36 to "Pitti" or walk from Ponte Vecchio in about 10 minutes.

2. Caffè Gilli
- **Address:** Via Roma, 1r, 50123 Florence
- **Price:** Cocktails from €10, Coffee from €3-€6
- **Why You Should Visit:** Established in 1733, Caffè Gilli is one of Florence's oldest and most elegant cafés. While it's more well-

known for its coffee, the bar here serves some of the finest cocktails in town. Located just off Piazza della Repubblica, it has a gorgeous setting, ideal for a relaxing evening or an afternoon aperitif. The polished, historic interiors paired with the marble counters and chandeliers give you a taste of Florence's old-world charm.
- **Activities:** Cocktails, aperitivo hour
- **How to Get There:** It's right by Piazza della Repubblica, a 5-minute walk from the Duomo. Easily accessible via bus or on foot.

3. Le Volpi e l'Uva
- **Address:** Piazza dei Rossi, 1, 50125 Florence
- **Price:** Glasses of wine from €5, bottles from €25.
- **Why You Should Visit:** A hidden gem tucked away on the edge of the Ponte Vecchio, Le Volpi e l'Uva specializes in artisanal wines from all over Italy. The rustic yet chic wine bar offers a small but carefully curated selection of wines, making it an ideal stop for those who enjoy tasting something a little more unique. They focus on natural wines, which are less processed and more about showcasing the purity of the grape.

On my last visit, I tried a glass of Chianti Classico that had just the right balance of acidity and fruitiness—perfect for pairing with their cheeses or prosciutto.
- **Activities:** Wine by the glass or bottle, food pairings
- **How to Get There:** It's located in the Oltrarno district, a short walk from the Ponte Vecchio (10 minutes).

4. The Lion's Fountain
- **Address:** Via della Pergola, 18, 50121 Florence
- **Price:** Draft beers from €5, cocktails from €8
- **Why You Should Visit:** For a more relaxed vibe, The Lion's Fountain offers an English-style pub experience in the heart of Florence. It's popular with locals and tourists alike, known for its large selection of international beers, cocktails, and hearty pub

food. Whether you're looking to watch a sports game or enjoy a quiet pint, the pub has a cozy, welcoming atmosphere.
If you're into classic cocktails, try their signature "Florence Old Fashioned"— it's a unique twist on the classic, with a local flair.
- **Activities:** Pub food, beer, sports on TV
- **How to Get There:** From Piazza della Signoria, it's a short walk (7 minutes). You can also take bus 23 to "Sant'Ambrogio."

5. Buca Lapi
- **Address:** Via del Trebbio, 1r, 50123 Florence
- **Price:** Cocktails around €10, wine by glass starting at €6.
- **Why You Should Visit:** This is one of Florence's most iconic spots, offering a blend of history and good drinks. Buca Lapi is actually located in the former cellar of Palazzo Vecchio, so you're essentially sipping wine in a centuries-old space that once served the aristocrats of Florence. It's been around since 1880 and is still beloved by locals.

What makes it unique, aside from the historic setting, is its warm, inviting atmosphere. Whether you want a refreshing glass of Prosecco or a robust red, Buca Lapi delivers. It's especially great if you're looking to explore the rich history of Florence while enjoying a drink.
- **Activities:** Wine tasting, intimate evening drinks
- **How to Get There:** Located a short walk from Piazza del Duomo.

6. Trattoria La Casalinga
- **Address:** Via de' Michelozzi, 9, 50125 Florence
- **Price:** Aperitivo from €6, wines from €5.
- **Why You Should Visit:** While primarily a traditional Florentine trattoria, La Casalinga has a wonderful little wine bar in its back corner. The selection includes some of the finest Tuscan wines, including local Chiantis and Vino Nobile di Montepulciano. You can enjoy a drink while sampling their famous ribollita soup or a classic Florentine steak.

A personal favorite: their light, floral white wine from the region of Vernaccia di San Gimignano pairs beautifully with the local cheese plate.

- **Activities:** Wine by the glass, pairing with traditional dishes.
- **How to Get There:** Located in the Oltrarno area, near the Santo Spirito neighborhood (10-minute walk from Ponte Vecchio).

Nightclubs, Live Music, and Jazz Clubs

However, the city boasts an eclectic and vibrant range of venues for music lovers and night owls alike. Whether you're looking to dance the night away at a nightclub, enjoy a live band, or relax with a glass of wine at a cozy jazz club, Florence has something to offer. Here's a guide to some of the best spots to explore, where the music flows as freely as the wine.

1. Central Park Club
- **Address**: Via Cavour, 80, 50129 Florence
- **Activities**: Dance club, themed nights, DJ performances
- **Price**: Entry €10-€15 (includes a drink)
- **Why Visit**: Located just a short walk from the historic center, Central Park Club is one of Florence's most popular nightclubs. Known for its modern, stylish atmosphere, it features international DJs and a mix of electronic, house, and pop music. The club hosts themed nights throughout the week, ensuring there's always something fresh and exciting. If you're in the mood for dancing, this is the place to be. Expect an energetic crowd and plenty of opportunities to let loose.

Pro Tip: Dress code is smart-casual, and arriving early might help you avoid long lines at the entrance.

2. Jazz Club Firenze
- **Address**: Via dei Pucci, 4, 50122 Florence
- **Activities**: Live jazz performances, jam sessions
- **Price**: €10-€20 depending on the performance
- **Why Visit**: If jazz is your thing, Jazz Club Firenze offers an intimate setting where world-class musicians perform nightly. It's a favorite among locals and tourists who want to experience live jazz in a relaxed, welcoming environment. The club's cozy interior,

with low lighting and a casual vibe, provides the perfect backdrop for a night of live music. Many evenings feature jam sessions where you can enjoy talented musicians improvising and collaborating.

Pro Tip: Get there early for a good seat—this place can fill up quickly, especially on weekends.

3. Tenax
- **Address**: Via Pratese, 46, 50127 Florence
- **Activities**: Nightclub, electronic music, live performances
- **Price**: Entry €10-€20 depending on the night
- **Why Visit**: Tenax is one of Florence's legendary nightclubs, known for its cutting-edge electronic music scene. With its dark, industrial setting and state-of-the-art sound system, Tenax attracts both local and international DJs and performers. This is the spot for those who want to dance to techno, house, and electronic beats. The crowd here is youthful and energetic, and the atmosphere is always electric.

Pro Tip: If you're into underground electronic music, check their event calendar in advance, as Tenax often hosts special events with big-name DJs.

4. La Menagere
- **Address**: Via de' Ginori, 8, 50123 Florence
- **Activities**: Live music, DJ sets, cocktails
- **Price**: Entry free (drinks are €8-€12)
- **Why Visit**: La Menagere is one of Florence's trendiest spots, offering a mix of live music, art, and fantastic cocktails. Located in a beautifully restored 19th-century building, this venue has an industrial-chic vibe with a café, restaurant, and bar all under one roof. While it's not exclusively a music venue, they often host live jazz, acoustic performances, and DJ sets, making it a great spot for a night out. The ambiance is relaxed, yet sophisticated, perfect for those who want to enjoy live music with a drink in hand.

Pro Tip: If you're in the mood for food, La Menagere has an excellent menu, with a variety of tapas and shareable plates to complement your evening.

5. Odeon Firenze
- **Address**: Piazza Strozzi, 50123 Florence
- **Activities**: Live jazz and classical music performances
- **Price**: Ticket prices vary for events, around €10-€30
- **Why Visit**: For a truly unique experience, head to Odeon Firenze, a stunning art deco cinema that doubles as a concert hall. While primarily known for its film screenings, the Odeon regularly hosts live jazz performances and classical concerts. The venue's beautiful, historic setting—complete with velvet seats and ornate decor—adds an elegant touch to any night out. If you're seeking a more sophisticated night, the Odeon offers the perfect mix of culture and entertainment.

Pro Tip: Check the event schedule ahead of time, as the venue often offers live performances tied to special exhibitions or film events.

6. Combo Social Club
- **Address**: Via Mannelli, 2, 50100 Florence
- **Activities**: Live music, art exhibitions, DJs
- **Price**: Free entry, drinks priced at €5-€8
- **Why Visit**: Combo Social Club is a lively and dynamic space, combining music, art, and social interaction. They regularly host a range of events, including live music performances, art exhibitions, and DJ sets. The venue has a laid-back, creative vibe and is perfect for those looking to experience Florence's modern arts scene. It's also a great spot to meet other travelers and locals while enjoying good music and cocktails.

Pro Tip: The club is located in the Santa Croce district, so it's easy to grab a late-night snack or enjoy a stroll through the historic area after the music winds down.

Why You Should Visit Florence's Nightlife Spots
Florence's nightlife scene may not rival that of cities like Berlin or Barcelona, but it offers something more intimate and charming. Whether you're a jazz aficionado, a nightclub enthusiast, or someone simply looking for a fun night out, Florence delivers experiences that feel personal and genuine. From cozy jazz bars tucked in narrow alleys to large, pulsating nightclubs that draw big crowds, there's a perfect spot for everyone.
In Florence, music is part of the city's fabric, and the venues reflect the city's blend of tradition and modernity. No matter where you go, you're bound to find a place that suits your mood, offering an unforgettable night of entertainment in the heart of Italy's cultural capital.
Pro Tip: Many venues in Florence require reservations for specific events or performances, so it's a good idea to check ahead of time, especially on weekends.

Rooftop Views: Evening Spots with a View of Florence

As the sun sets behind the rolling Tuscan hills, the city transforms, casting a golden glow on its terracotta rooftops and iconic monuments. Whether you're sipping an aperitivo or simply enjoying the view, these elevated spots offer an unforgettable experience. Let's explore a few of the best rooftop venues in Florence where you can drink in both the stunning views and the city's timeless charm.

1. La Terrazza Lounge Bar at Hotel Continentale
- **Address:** Via Porta Rossa 7, 50123 Florence
- **Price:** Cocktails range from €12-€18
- **Why Visit:** This rooftop bar, located at the stylish Hotel Continentale, offers one of the most breathtaking panoramic views of Florence. From here, you can admire the iconic Duomo, the Ponte Vecchio, and the rolling hills in the distance. It's the perfect spot to watch the sunset with a cocktail in hand, and the intimate

ambiance makes it ideal for couples or anyone looking to relax after a day of sightseeing.

Real-Life Example: I remember visiting La Terrazza during my last trip to Florence. The staff were incredibly welcoming, and as I sat back on the plush couches, sipping on an Aperol Spritz, the sky turned a brilliant shade of orange. The view of the Duomo with its dome illuminated against the evening sky was nothing short of magical. If you're a fan of photography, this is an ideal spot to snap some unforgettable shots of Florence from above.

2. SE·STO on Arno
- **Address:** Lungarno della Zecca Vecchia 38, 50122 Florence
- **Price:** Starters from €20, main courses from €35, cocktails from €15
- **Why Visit:** Located on the top floor of the luxurious Hotel The Westin Excelsior, SE·STO on Arno is one of Florence's most upscale rooftop bars and restaurants. Offering 360-degree views of the city, you can take in Florence's major landmarks, including the Arno River, Ponte Vecchio, and the distant Tuscan countryside. It's a great place to enjoy a refined dinner or cocktails as you watch the sunset. The sophisticated atmosphere is perfect for a special night out.

Personal Anecdote: I had dinner here one evening, and the combination of incredible food and an unforgettable view made for one of the highlights of my Florence trip. The sunset over the Arno was mesmerizing, and I found myself lost in the scenery, all while enjoying an exquisite Tuscan wine pairing with my meal. If you're in the mood for luxury, this is the place to be.

3. Rooftop Bar at Hotel Brunelleschi
- **Address:** Piazza San Firenze 3, 50122 Florence
- **Price:** Cocktails from €10-€16
- **Why Visit:** Nestled in the heart of the city, Hotel Brunelleschi's rooftop bar offers a fantastic view of the Duomo and the Florence skyline. The setting is a bit more casual compared to the others, which makes it an excellent choice if you're looking for a laid-back

place to enjoy a drink with friends. The best part? The historical backdrop. The hotel is built into a former Byzantine tower, adding a layer of history to the evening's atmosphere.

Practical Tip: The rooftop bar gets especially busy around sunset, so try to arrive early to secure a spot by the edge of the terrace. The staff are friendly and attentive, and they often serve complimentary small bites with your drinks, which is always a nice touch.

4. Caffè degli Artigiani
- **Address:** Via dei Neri 47r, 50122 Florence
- **Price:** Cocktails range from €10-€14
- **Why Visit:** For a more local experience, head to Caffè degli Artigiani. Although not as high up as some other rooftops, the small but charming rooftop terrace offers great views of the city center. This place is popular with Florentines, making it a more relaxed and authentic spot compared to the tourist-heavy venues. It's also known for its craft cocktails made with locally sourced ingredients, so it's perfect for cocktail lovers.

Real-Life Example: I stumbled upon this rooftop bar while wandering through the historic center. It's a hidden gem, and I could tell from the mix of locals and visitors that it was a beloved spot. The bartender crafted a unique cocktail for me using lavender from the Tuscan countryside. Sitting on the terrace as the city buzzed below was a wonderfully peaceful experience, and the intimate vibe made it feel like a true Florentine evening.

5. The Roof at Hotel Minerva
- **Address:** Piazza di Santa Maria Novella 16, 50123 Florence
- **Price:** Drinks from €8-€12
- **Why Visit:** Situated in Piazza Santa Maria Novella, this rooftop bar offers one of the best views of the historic center. From here, you can take in views of the cathedral, the hills surrounding Florence, and the city's iconic skyline. The atmosphere is casual yet chic, making it a great choice for unwinding after a day of sightseeing or grabbing a quick drink before heading to dinner. The terrace is

also known for its relaxed vibe and reasonable prices, making it a favorite among tourists and locals alike.
Practical Tip: The rooftop is open to both guests and non-guests of the hotel, but it's especially popular in the summer months, so be sure to reserve a table if you're visiting during peak times. The panoramic view combined with a cool breeze in the evening makes it a fantastic spot to enjoy Florence's beauty.

Why You Should Visit Rooftop Bars in Florence
Florence's rooftops offer more than just a drink; they offer a chance to see the city in a new light. There's something enchanting about sipping a drink while watching the sun dip behind the hills, casting its warm light over the historic monuments. Whether you're a history buff, a photographer, or simply someone who appreciates a beautiful view, the city's rooftop terraces provide an experience you won't soon forget.

How to Get There: Most of these rooftop bars are easily accessible by foot from the city center. Florence is a pedestrian-friendly city, so you can enjoy walking from one stunning spot to the next.

Theaters and Performance Spaces

Theaters in Florence have a long and storied history, offering everything from classic opera to contemporary drama, and even local performances that reflect the city's vibrant arts scene. Whether you're a fan of grand performances in historic venues or prefer something a bit more intimate, Florence has something to offer every theater lover.

1. Teatro della Pergola
One of the oldest and most prestigious theaters in Florence, Teatro della Pergola has been entertaining audiences since the 17th century. Located in the heart of the city, this theater is a must-see for anyone interested in Florence's theatrical history.
Address: Via della Pergola, 12, 50121 Florence
How to Get There: It's easily accessible by walking from the historic

center. If you're staying near the Duomo, it's about a 10-minute walk. Alternatively, take the ATAF bus lines 6 or 14 and get off at the "S. Annunziata" stop.
Why Visit: The theater itself is a work of art, with its beautiful frescoes, red velvet seats, and intimate atmosphere. It's known for hosting a wide variety of performances, including classic Italian opera, ballet, and contemporary plays. The acoustics are superb, making it a favorite spot for both performers and audiences.
Activities: Teatro della Pergola regularly features opera, ballet, and theater productions. It's particularly famous for its opera festivals, showcasing works by composers like Verdi and Puccini. If you're in town during the fall or winter, be sure to check out their seasonal programming, which often includes Italian-language productions.
Price: Ticket prices vary depending on the production, ranging from €20 to €80. There are also special discounts for students and senior citizens.

2. Teatro Verdi
Another iconic theater in Florence, Teatro Verdi is known for its opera and concert performances. Located in the San Frediano district, it offers a more modern take on the traditional theater experience, with an emphasis on musical performances.
Address: Via Ghibellina, 99, 50122 Florence
How to Get There: A 15-minute walk from the Piazza del Duomo or a short tram ride (Tram Line T1) to the "Palazzo di Giustizia" stop.
Why Visit: Teatro Verdi is the place to go for opera lovers, with regular performances ranging from classic operas to more modern musical theater. The venue is also home to concerts featuring both Italian and international artists. The atmosphere here is more contemporary, yet it still carries the elegance of Florence's cultural heritage.
Activities: Aside from opera, Teatro Verdi hosts symphonic concerts, chamber music, and contemporary performances. It's an excellent venue for those looking to experience a mix of high culture and modern musical innovation.

Price: Tickets typically range from €30 to €70 depending on the performance. Discounts are available for students and seniors, and there are often special deals for early bookings.

3. Stabilimento delle Arti (Art Factory)
For something a little different, head to Stabilimento delle Arti, a contemporary performance space that focuses on innovative and experimental theater. Located in a former industrial space, it's known for pushing the boundaries of traditional performance art.
Address: Via dei Gori, 10, 50127 Florence
How to Get There: It's located in the Santa Croce area, and it's best accessed via bus (Line 14) or a 15-minute walk from the Santa Croce church.
Why Visit: This is a great spot for those interested in avant-garde performances and contemporary theater. Stabilimento delle Arti showcases works from both Italian and international artists, often with a focus on social issues and interactive experiences. It's also a fantastic place to experience new forms of live art, such as immersive theater or multimedia performances.
Activities: You'll find performances that range from experimental plays to live art installations, as well as workshops and talks from the artists themselves. It's an ideal place for those seeking something out of the ordinary and willing to embrace the cutting-edge world of modern theater.
Price: Entry prices vary depending on the performance but are generally around €15 to €25. Some events are even free, especially for local residents.

4. Opera di Firenze (Opera House of Florence)
For a truly grand and classical experience, the Opera di Firenze is a world-class venue offering top-tier opera and ballet performances. This is Florence's modern answer to the grand opera houses of Europe, and it's a must-visit for fans of the performing arts.
Address: Corso Italia, 16, 50122 Florence
How to Get There: A 20-minute walk from the historic center, or take bus 14 or 23 to the "Ricasoli" stop.

Why Visit: The Opera di Firenze is one of the best places to experience grand opera and ballet in Florence. The acoustics in the auditorium are phenomenal, and the building itself is a marvel of modern architecture, blending contemporary design with traditional opera house elements. The performances here feature world-class artists and conductors, often showcasing the best of Italian and international talent.

Activities: Expect performances of classic operas like *La Traviata* or *Carmen*, as well as seasonal ballet productions. The venue is also known for hosting international orchestras and symphonic concerts, making it a key stop for any music lover visiting Florence.

Price: Tickets range from €20 to €100 depending on the production. There are often discounted tickets for students, seniors, and groups, and some performances offer reduced rates for residents.

Practical Tips for Theatergoers in Florence

- **Check Schedules in Advance**: Florence's theaters often have seasonal programs, so it's a good idea to check the schedules online before you travel. Many theaters also offer discounts or special events, so keep an eye out for deals.
- **Dress Code**: While Florence's theaters don't have a strict dress code, it's always a good idea to dress smartly when attending a performance, especially in venues like Teatro della Pergola or the Opera di Firenze.
- **Language**: Most performances are in Italian, but some theaters offer subtitles or translations. Be sure to check if the production you're attending offers this option.

Seasonal Nighttime Events

From festivals celebrating art and music to unique cultural experiences, here's a look at some of the most exciting seasonal nighttime events in Florence.

Florence Summer Festival (Firenze Summer Festival)

Every summer, Florence hosts the *Firenze Summer Festival*, a series of open-air concerts that draw big names from the world of pop, jazz, and classical music. This event is perfect for music lovers looking to enjoy a night under the stars while listening to international artists in a spectacular setting.

- **Location:** Various venues, including the *Piazza Santa Croce* and *Teatro Verdi*.
- **When:** Usually runs from June to July.
- **Price:** Tickets vary, but typically range from €20-€70 depending on the artist and venue.
- **Why You Should Visit:** Imagine listening to a live concert with the beautiful Florence skyline in the background. It's an experience that blends culture, music, and the city's stunning atmosphere.
- **How to Get There:** Central venues like *Piazza Santa Croce* are easily accessible by foot from most city center locations. For further venues, public transport or taxis are recommended.

Calcio Storico (Historic Football)

One of the most unique and historically significant events in Florence, *Calcio Storico* is a mix of soccer, rugby, and wrestling, played in medieval Florentine fashion. This ancient game is played every June in celebration of the Feast of St. John, the city's patron saint. Though the event happens during the day, the atmosphere during the evening celebrations is electric, with live music, processions, and a festive vibe that fills the city.

- **Location:** *Piazza Santa Croce* (the main playing field).
- **When:** June 24th (Feast of St. John).
- **Price:** Spectator tickets for the final game range from €25-€50, though the public celebrations are free.
- **Why You Should Visit:** Watching the game is an incredible experience, but the evening festivities—complete with parades and fireworks—offer a true taste of Florence's vibrant, historic culture. It's an event like no other.
- **How to Get There:** *Piazza Santa Croce* is centrally located and easily reachable by foot or public transport.

Florence Light Festival

The *Florence Light Festival* illuminates the city with stunning installations and light shows during the winter months. Held every year in December, this festival showcases cutting-edge light art, projecting large-scale installations onto Florence's historic landmarks, bridges, and buildings.

- **Location:** Various iconic locations including *Ponte Vecchio*, *Piazza del Duomo*, and *Piazza della Signoria*.
- **When:** Mid-December to early January.
- **Price:** Free to the public.
- **Why You Should Visit:** Florence's art and architecture take on a whole new dimension when illuminated by these spectacular light displays. Whether you're admiring the Duomo bathed in light or walking along the Arno River with glowing sculptures all around you, the ambiance is unforgettable.
- **How to Get There:** The installations are scattered throughout the city center, so walking is the best way to experience them. If you're staying further out, hop on a bus or tram for easy access.

Pitti Immagine Uomo and Fashion Nights

Florence is renowned for its fashion, and *Pitti Immagine Uomo*—the world's most important fashion event for menswear—takes place twice a year in June and January. While most activities are held during the day, the evening events are a highlight, with exclusive parties, pop-up shows, and live music events.

- **Location:** *Fortezza da Basso* and select venues around the city.
- **When:** Mid-June and Mid-January.
- **Price:** Ticket prices for shows and parties vary. Entry to the general exhibition area is usually around €30-€50.
- **Why You Should Visit:** If you love fashion, the night events during *Pitti Immagine Uomo* are a chance to mix with the fashion elite. Expect glamorous cocktail parties, private shows, and opportunities to see the latest trends.

- **How to Get There:** The *Fortezza da Basso* is a short walk from *Santa Maria Novella* train station, or you can take a bus if you're staying further out.

Festa della Rificolana (Festival of Lanterns)

Held every September, the *Festa della Rificolana* is a colorful festival where locals celebrate with handmade paper lanterns, music, and a vibrant parade. Children and adults alike take to the streets with their lanterns, lighting up the night in a stunning display of Florentine tradition.

- **Location:** *Piazza Santissima Annunziata* and the streets of Florence.
- **When:** The first week of September.
- **Price:** Free to watch, though some events like the lantern-making workshops may have a small fee.
- **Why You Should Visit:** This event captures the essence of Florence's charming, traditional side. It's a fantastic way to see the city from a local perspective, filled with warmth and community spirit.
- **How to Get There:** The main events take place in the city center, so walking is your best bet. Buses and trams can also get you close.

Florence Christmas Markets and Events

Florence transforms into a winter wonderland during the Christmas season, with Christmas markets popping up throughout the city. The most famous is the *German Christmas Market* in *Piazza Santa Croce*, but other parts of the city host festive light displays, ice skating rinks, and holiday concerts.

- **Location:** *Piazza Santa Croce* and other areas like *Piazza del Duomo*.
- **When:** Late November to early January.
- **Price:** Free to visit markets, though items and activities (like ice skating) will have fees.
- **Why You Should Visit:** The festive lights, smells of mulled wine and roasted chestnuts, and holiday cheer make Florence's

Christmas events feel extra special. The atmosphere is cozy and welcoming, perfect for getting into the holiday spirit.
- **How to Get There:** The Christmas markets and events are all within walking distance of the historic city center. If you're further out, use public transport.

Florence's seasonal nighttime events give you the chance to experience the city's charm in a way that few other cities can match. From celebrating ancient traditions to admiring modern light art, these events bring Florence's artistic, cultural, and festive sides to life.

Tips for a Night Out in Florence

Florence has something to offer. Here are some practical tips and recommendations for making the most of your night out in the city.

1. Start with Aperitivo – The Florentine Way

In Florence, the evening usually begins with **aperitivo**, a beloved tradition where you can enjoy a drink and complimentary snacks before dinner. This is an excellent way to soak up the atmosphere of the city while trying some local specialties. You'll find aperitivo offerings throughout the city, particularly in the historic center.

One of my favorite spots for aperitivo is **La Terrazza**, a rooftop bar with a fantastic view of the Arno River and Ponte Vecchio. It's a perfect place to enjoy a spritz and catch the sunset. The drink prices might be a little higher here, but the atmosphere makes it worthwhile. Another great option is **Caffè Gilli**, a historic café on Piazza della Repubblica, where you can enjoy a more elegant vibe with a selection of bite-sized treats alongside your cocktail.

Pro Tip: If you're on a budget, look for bars that offer an aperitivo buffet for the price of a drink. Many places in Florence, especially in the San Lorenzo area, will serve a generous spread of pasta, meats, cheeses, and even pizza!

2. Stroll the Historic Streets for an Evening Experience

Florence is small enough to explore on foot, and there's something magical about the way the city looks when it's illuminated by streetlights. Take a stroll along the **Ponte Vecchio** to see the jewelry shops glowing in the dark or wander through **Piazza del Duomo** to admire the cathedral's stunning façade lit up at night. These iconic spots are just as breathtaking at night as they are during the day.

I've always found that a walk around the **Piazza della Signoria** at night is one of Florence's most underrated experiences. The statues in the square, including **Michelangelo's David** (the copy— the original is in the Accademia), come alive with the night lighting. It's a peaceful time to reflect on the history around you, minus the daytime crowds.

3. Discover the Best Bars and Clubs

Florence has a variety of bars and clubs catering to all tastes. Whether you prefer cozy, intimate places or high-energy spots to dance the night away, you'll find a place that suits your style.

Colle Bereto, located in Piazza degli Strozzi, is a stylish bar that locals love for its cocktails and chic atmosphere. It's a great place to start your night out, especially if you're after a mix of relaxed sophistication and a touch of glamour. For something a bit more lively, head to **Central Park**, one of the city's most famous nightclubs. It's located just outside the historic center but is worth the trip for its international crowd and dance beats.

Pro Tip: If you're into craft cocktails, make sure to check out **The Fusion Bar** in the Santa Croce area. It's a hidden gem, perfect for those looking for expertly crafted drinks and a cool, laid-back vibe.

4. Late-Night Pizza and Gelato Stops

Florence may be known for its museums and art, but after a few drinks, there's nothing better than grabbing a late-night slice of pizza. One of the best places to do this is **Gusta Pizza**, near the **Santo Spirito** neighborhood. Their wood-fired pizzas are delicious and served up quickly, making it the perfect late-night snack after a few drinks at the nearby bars.

For those with a sweet tooth, Florence is home to some incredible gelato shops, many of which stay open well into the night. **Gelateria dei Neri**, located near the Uffizi Gallery, is a must-visit for its rich, creamy flavors. I'll never forget enjoying a cone of pistachio gelato on a warm evening while walking along the Arno River.

5. Enjoy Florence's Music Scene

Florence's music scene is diverse, offering everything from jazz to electronic beats. If you're a fan of live music, check out **Jazz Club Firenze** near Piazza del Carmine. This cozy, intimate venue hosts regular jazz performances, giving you the opportunity to enjoy a night of great music in a relaxed setting.

For something more upbeat, head to **Tenax**, one of the best nightclubs in the city for electronic music and live DJ sets. It's a bit further from the center but worth it if you're looking to dance until the early morning hours. Many of the local clubs host themed nights, so be sure to check the calendar before you go.

6. Relax and Unwind with Night Views

If you're looking to wind down after a night of socializing, Florence offers some stunning spots where you can enjoy a peaceful drink while gazing out over the city. **Piazzale Michelangelo**, a large square that offers panoramic views of Florence, is a perfect place to reflect on your day. There's a small café where you can enjoy a nightcap while watching the city below, which feels almost surreal as the lights shimmer off the historic buildings.

Another quiet place to enjoy Florence by night is **Fiesole**, a hilltop town just outside the city. You can catch a bus or a short taxi ride from the center and find a peaceful bar overlooking Florence—it's a more tranquil escape from the bustle of the city.

7. Respect Local Customs

Florentines take their nightlife seriously, but they also enjoy a balance between relaxation and socializing. Unlike some other cities, Florence doesn't have a "party until dawn" culture, and many places start to close by 2 a.m. This is especially true on weekdays, so if you want to experience Florence's nightlife fully, start early and take your time.

Remember to also be respectful of the locals. Florence's historical center can get crowded, and the narrow streets can become quite lively at night. Keep an eye on your belongings and be mindful of noise levels, especially in the residential areas.

Shopping in Florence

Fashion Boutiques and Local Designers

As the birthplace of the Italian Renaissance, it's no surprise that the city's boutiques and local designers continue to uphold the traditions of artistry, craftsmanship, and sophistication. Walking through the narrow cobblestone streets, you'll find a blend of modern and vintage fashion that perfectly captures the essence of Italian elegance. Whether you're on the hunt for high-end designer pieces or unique artisan-made treasures, Florence offers something for every fashion lover.

1. Via de' Tornabuoni:

One of the most renowned shopping streets in Florence is Via de' Tornabuoni, where luxury boutiques line the historic street. Here, you'll find flagship stores for high-end brands like Gucci, Prada, and Ferragamo. But what's even more exciting for fashion enthusiasts are the local designers who also call this street home. For example, **Lorenzo Villoresi**, a boutique dedicated to Florence's famed perfumer, offers a blend of timeless scents and bespoke fashion accessories. Prices vary depending on the item, with scarves and ties starting around €150.

Address: Via de' Tornabuoni 56r, 50123 Florence
Where to Buy: Via de' Tornabuoni or online at Lorenzo Villoresi's official website.

2. Santa Maria Novella:

For those looking to explore Florence's more traditional style, the **Santa Maria Novella Pharmacy** (Officina Profumo-Farmaceutica di Santa Maria Novella) is not only a great stop for perfumes but also a treasure trove for luxurious clothing and accessories. Although known primarily for its rich history as one of the oldest pharmacies in the world, the store carries an elegant range of hand-crafted leather goods, clothing, and textiles—each item echoing Florence's history of artisan craftsmanship.

Address: Via della Scala 16, 50123 Florence
Price: Leather goods such as wallets or belts range from €100 to €300, while scarves and apparel vary.

3. The Oltrarno District:
On the quieter, more bohemian side of Florence, the **Oltrarno District** is home to an array of boutique shops featuring independent designers and artisans. This area offers the chance to explore unique, one-of-a-kind pieces. One standout is **Margarita Barrocas**, a designer known for her handmade leather handbags. Margarita's bags combine traditional Tuscan leatherwork with contemporary designs, offering pieces that are both functional and beautiful. Expect to pay between €200 and €500 for a high-quality bag.
Address: Via dei Serragli 40r, 50124 Florence
Where to Buy: In-store or directly from Margarita Barrocas' website.

4. Pitti Uomo:
Florence is also home to **Pitti Uomo**, one of the world's most influential men's fashion events, held biannually. Pitti Uomo showcases both established and up-and-coming local designers, making it a must-visit for those interested in contemporary Italian menswear. Beyond the event, Florence has a number of boutiques offering exclusive men's fashion lines. **Camoshita** is one example. Known for its high-end menswear with a modern twist, Camoshita's collections feature Italian craftsmanship paired with Japanese design elements. Expect to find blazers, shirts, and trousers starting at €200.
Address: Via dei Ginori 5r, 50123 Florence
Price: Shirts start at €150, suits around €500.

5. Carlo Cecchini:
Florence is renowned for its leather goods, and **Carlo Cecchini** is one of the finest examples of a local designer who keeps the tradition alive with contemporary flair. Known for his high-quality leather shoes, bags, and accessories, Carlo Cecchini's boutique features beautifully crafted designs made from the finest Italian leather. His creations are timeless yet fashion-

forward, with pieces that are perfect for both casual and formal wear. Prices for leather handbags or shoes start at around €150, while bespoke pieces can go up to €500 or more.
Address: Via dei Magazzini 2r, 50123 Florence
Where to Buy: In-store or via Carlo Cecchini's official online store.

6. Luisa Via Roma:
For those looking for a luxurious fashion experience that still has a local touch, **Luisa Via Roma** is a Florence institution. Although it carries international designer brands, it also champions a select group of local Italian designers who specialize in avant-garde fashion. The store frequently collaborates with local artisans and hosts exclusive collections. Here, you can find everything from elegant evening wear to street style chic. Prices vary widely, with contemporary Italian designer shoes starting at €250 and dresses from €600 upwards.
Address: Via Roma 1r, 50123 Florence
Price: Shoes start at €250, dresses at €600, and handbags can exceed €1,000.

7. Sergio Rossi:
Known globally for its luxurious, handcrafted shoes, **Sergio Rossi** is one of the finest examples of Italian craftsmanship. While the brand has an international presence, its boutique in Florence is a perfect place to pick up a pair of shoes that combine elegance, comfort, and style. Here, you can find everything from sleek stilettos to chic boots, all made with precision and quality. Expect to pay from €300 to €1,000 for a pair of shoes, depending on the style.
Address: Via della Vigna Nuova 22r, 50123 Florence
Where to Buy: In-store or online through Sergio Rossi's website.

Tips for Shopping in Florence
- **Be prepared for the crowds**: Florence is a popular destination for tourists, so try to visit boutiques early in the morning or later in the afternoon to avoid large crowds.

- **Look for craftsmanship**: Florence's local designers pride themselves on handmade quality. Many of the boutiques offer custom-made pieces, allowing you to take home something truly unique.
- **Don't forget about leather**: Italy is known for its high-quality leather, and Florence is one of the best places to shop for it. From jackets to bags to shoes, you'll find beautiful leather goods all around the city.

Artisan Shops and Unique Souvenirs

Whether you're seeking a beautiful leather bag, a hand-painted ceramic plate, or a piece of Florentine gold jewelry, the city's artisan shops offer a world of craftsmanship that tells the story of its Renaissance roots. Here's a guide to some of the best places to find truly special items that will bring a piece of Florence home with you.

1. Florentine Leather Goods

Florence has been known for its leather craftsmanship for centuries, and a piece of locally-made leather is one of the most sought-after souvenirs in the city. The leather artisans in Florence use centuries-old techniques to create stunning bags, belts, wallets, and jackets that are crafted from the finest Italian leather.

Where to buy:
- *Scuola del Cuoio* (Via San Giuseppe, 5r) – This workshop is located near the Santa Croce Basilica and is renowned for its high-quality leather goods. You can witness artisans at work and purchase anything from handbags to wallets, all handmade and personalized with your choice of design.
- **Price Range:** Small leather items like wallets start around €40, while larger items like bags and jackets can range from €100 to €500.
- **Tip:** Don't miss the opportunity to have your leather bag customized with your initials for an extra personal touch!

2. Hand-Painted Ceramics

Florence is home to many skilled ceramic artists who create hand-painted plates, bowls, vases, and decorative items that reflect the beauty of the Tuscan landscape. These ceramics are not just decorative; they often depict traditional Florentine motifs like the fleur-de-lis, rich in history and symbolism.

Where to buy:
- *Ceramiche San Lorenzo* (Via de' Cerretani, 47r) – Located near the San Lorenzo Market, this family-run ceramic shop offers a wide selection of hand-painted pieces, from large dinner plates to intricate pottery.
- **Price Range:** Small plates start at around €30, while larger items can cost up to €100 or more.
- **Tip:** Consider picking up a hand-painted tile as a unique keepsake to hang in your home—it's both beautiful and practical!

3. Florentine Gold Jewelry

Florence has long been a center of goldsmithing, and the gold jewelry found here is unlike anything you'll find elsewhere. The Ponte Vecchio, with its charming jewelry shops, is the best place to pick up a memorable piece of Florentine craftsmanship. Whether it's a traditional gold chain or a modern design, the quality and attention to detail are unparalleled.

Where to buy:
- *Frosini Gioielli* (Ponte Vecchio, 39r) – Located on the famous bridge, Frosini is a respected goldsmith that offers exquisite jewelry, from classic gold rings to bold modern designs.
- **Price Range:** Gold rings start at around €100, and more intricate pieces like necklaces can range from €200 to €1,000 or more.
- **Tip:** Buying from the Ponte Vecchio means you're getting a piece of history with your purchase, as the shops have been family-owned for generations.

4. Handmade Paper and Stationery

Florence's tradition of paper making dates back centuries, and you can find beautiful hand-crafted paper goods throughout the city. These items make for thoughtful, elegant souvenirs—whether you're picking up a hand-bound journal or a set of unique letterpress prints.

Where to buy:
- *Il Papiro* (Via dei Neri, 58r) – This charming shop is a local favorite for high-quality handmade paper, journals, stationery, and more. The paper is often made using ancient Florentine techniques, making each item truly special.
- **Price Range:** A small notebook starts at around €25, while a handcrafted stationary set can go for €40 to €60.
- **Tip:** If you're a writer or artist, pick up a journal made from Florentine paper as a perfect place to jot down your travels and memories.

5. Marbled Paper

Florence is also known for its stunning marbled paper, which has been a craft in the city since the Renaissance. These beautiful papers are often used for bookbinding, but you'll also find them in notebooks, decorative pieces, and stationery.

Where to buy:
- *Paperella* (Via dell'Olmo, 8r) – This small boutique offers an incredible selection of marbled papers, from vibrant colors to more subtle, earthy tones. You'll find everything from decorative marbled paper to unique book covers and writing materials.
- **Price Range:** A single sheet of marbled paper starts around €10, while notebooks and custom bookbinding services can cost from €30 to €100.
- **Tip:** Consider getting a custom-made journal bound in marbled paper for a truly unique and luxurious souvenir.

6. Handmade Wooden Products

Florence's artisan woodworkers create beautiful handcrafted products, ranging from simple wooden toys to intricate home decor. The use of local wood combined with skilled craftsmanship results in items that are both functional and artistic.

Where to buy:
- *Laboratorio del Legno* (Via delle Belle Donne, 35r) – This artisan workshop specializes in handcrafted wooden items like puzzles, decorative boxes, and custom-made furniture.
- **Price Range:** Small items like wooden toys or trinket boxes can start at €25, while larger pieces such as furniture can range from €150 to €1,000.
- **Tip:** If you're looking for something truly personal, you can commission a custom wooden piece, made specifically for you.

7. Tuscan Wines and Olive Oil
Florence and the surrounding Tuscan region are known for their wines and olive oil, both of which make excellent gifts. Local wineries and olive groves offer handcrafted bottles of wine and oil that are often produced using traditional, time-honored techniques.

Where to buy:
- *Enoteca Pitti Gola e Cantina* (Piazza Pitti, 16r) – This wine shop near the Pitti Palace offers a wide selection of local wines and olive oils, often from small, family-run producers in Tuscany.
- **Price Range:** A bottle of quality Tuscan olive oil starts around €15, while wines can range from €20 to €200, depending on the vineyard.
- **Tip:** Ask for recommendations based on your taste preferences— the staff here is knowledgeable and can guide you to the perfect bottle.

Leather Markets and Goldsmith Shops
The city's leather markets and goldsmith shops are essential stops for anyone looking to take a piece of the city's artisanal heritage home. Whether you're hunting for a stylish leather jacket or a unique piece of jewelry, Florence offers a rich blend of history, artistry, and shopping.

The Leather Market at San Lorenzo

Start your leather shopping adventure at the famous **San Lorenzo Market** (Piazza San Lorenzo, 50123 Florence). This bustling market is a must-visit for anyone interested in high-quality leather goods at relatively reasonable prices. The market is packed with leather jackets, handbags, belts, and wallets. Many of the vendors here are family-run businesses that have been perfecting their craft for generations.

Example: Florentine Leather Works

One of the standout shops in this market is **Florentine Leather Works**. It's an authentic family-owned business that specializes in bespoke leather jackets and bags. Prices here vary, but expect to pay around €150-€500 for a handmade leather jacket, depending on the style and intricacy of the design. If you're looking for something special, they offer customizations, so you can get exactly what you want, whether it's a soft, distressed leather or a more polished look.

What makes this market especially appealing is the chance to interact directly with the artisans. You can watch as they cut, sew, and stitch the leather, often providing insights into the traditional methods that have been passed down through generations. Don't hesitate to ask questions about the materials and processes – many of the artisans are happy to share their knowledge.

The Goldsmiths of Ponte Vecchio

The **Ponte Vecchio** (Piazza dei Pitti, 50125 Florence), a world-famous bridge that spans the Arno River, is not only a beautiful landmark but also home to an array of goldsmith shops. These tiny boutiques offer finely crafted jewelry that showcases Florence's long history of gold and silver work. If you're in the market for something luxurious and timeless, this is the place to be.

Example: Benvenuto Cellini

At **Benvenuto Cellini**, located just along the bridge, you'll find some of the best gold jewelry in Florence. Expect prices to start around €200 for a simple ring, with more elaborate designs ranging from €500 to well over €2,000. The shop is renowned for its high-end craftsmanship and attention to detail, creating pieces that are not just jewelry, but works of art.

If you're not sure what to buy, try a gold bracelet or a pendant. These items are perfect keepsakes, and many of the pieces are inspired by traditional Florentine designs, such as intricate floral patterns or historical symbols. Keep an eye out for their special collection of earrings, bracelets, and necklaces, often set with precious gemstones like diamonds or emeralds.

The Mercato Nuovo: A Leather Lover's Paradise
For a different leather experience, head to the **Mercato Nuovo** (Piazza del Mercato Nuovo, 50123 Florence), often referred to as the "Market of Straw." Although small, this market is filled with leather stalls that offer everything from jackets to sandals, often at more competitive prices than those found in the main tourist areas.

Example: La Pelle Firenze
A local favorite, **La Pelle Firenze**, specializes in handmade leather belts and wallets. Their designs are both functional and stylish, with prices ranging from €30 for a wallet to €100-€200 for a leather belt. The quality is exceptional, and the leather is soft but durable. Many customers return to purchase additional items after their first visit because the pieces are such great value.

While you're here, make sure to admire the **Porcellino** (a bronze boar statue) just outside the market. Legend has it that rubbing the boar's nose will bring you good luck – it's a fun tradition to participate in while shopping!

The Gold Shops of Via dei Calzaiuoli
Located near the **Piazza del Duomo**, **Via dei Calzaiuoli** is a charming street filled with boutiques selling luxury gold jewelry. This area is more sophisticated, with higher-end shops catering to a more exclusive clientele.

Example: Pasquale Bruni

At **Pasquale Bruni**, an iconic Florentine jewelry brand, you can find exquisite designs that combine traditional Italian artistry with contemporary elegance. Prices for a piece here can range from €500 for simple earrings to several thousand euros for elaborate necklaces and rings. The store is known for using innovative techniques and high-quality stones, making their collections some of the most desirable in Florence. The designs at Pasquale Bruni are inspired by nature, with motifs like flowers, leaves, and animals beautifully represented in each piece. If you're looking to splurge or buy a memorable gift, this shop is the place to go.

Leather and Gold Markets at Piazza del Duomo

The area around **Piazza del Duomo** offers a mix of both leather and gold markets, where you'll find a great selection of bags, shoes, and jewelry that reflect the city's artistic flair. It's also home to some of the more tourist-centric shops, which means prices can be higher, but the quality still meets the high standards Florence is known for.

Example: Il Bisonte

Il Bisonte (Piazza San Giovanni, 50123 Florence) is one of the most famous leather brands in Florence, known for its beautifully crafted bags and accessories. Prices here start at around €100 for small items like wallets and go up to €500 or more for large bags. The brand has a global following, so if you're looking for a stylish, high-quality souvenir that reflects the essence of Florence, this is a great place to visit.

Santa Croce and the Artisan Leather District

Finally, the **Santa Croce** district, just a short walk from the city center, is home to some of Florence's most renowned artisan workshops. This area isn't as crowded as the main tourist sites, making it an ideal spot to find unique, handmade leather goods.

Example: Scuola del Cuoio

For an authentic leather shopping experience, visit **Scuola del Cuoio** (Via San Giuseppe, 50122 Florence), an artisan leather workshop and school where leather goods are crafted by hand by skilled artisans. The prices here can be a bit steeper due to the quality and craftsmanship involved – expect to pay anywhere from €100 for a wallet to €500 for a jacket. What makes this place special is the opportunity to watch the artisans at work and even take a workshop to make your own leather goods.

High-End Shops in the Historic Center

Whether you're a seasoned shopper or just someone who appreciates fine craftsmanship, the historic center of Florence offers a unique opportunity to explore some of the best luxury boutiques in Italy. Here, we'll take a deep dive into the world of Florence's high-end shops—places where world-class artisanship meets Italian flair.

1. Gucci Garden

Address: Piazza della Signoria, 10, 50122 Florence, Italy
Price Range: Luxury goods starting around €500 for small leather accessories, up to several thousand for high-end clothing
What to Buy: Luxury fashion, bags, shoes, and exclusive Gucci collections
Gucci Garden, located right in the heart of Piazza della Signoria, is a must-visit for any fashion lover. This flagship store is more than just a boutique—it's a complete sensory experience. The space is designed as a combination of museum, showroom, and retail experience, allowing you to immerse yourself in the brand's unique aesthetic.
As you wander through the store, you'll find a curated selection of the latest Gucci collections, including bags, shoes, ready-to-wear, and the brand's iconic accessories. What makes Gucci Garden stand out, however, is its exclusive collections that can only be found in Florence. If you're looking for something truly unique, this is the place. Be sure to visit the adjacent restaurant and enjoy a meal in the same stylish surroundings!
Insider Tip: Keep an eye out for seasonal pop-up collections and limited-edition pieces that aren't available anywhere else.

2. Salvatore Ferragamo

Address: Via de' Tornabuoni, 2, 50123 Florence, Italy
Price Range: Leather goods starting from €300, shoes from €500, and high-end clothing from €1,000+
What to Buy: Shoes, leather bags, belts, and accessories

Salvatore Ferragamo's flagship store is a tribute to one of Italy's most iconic fashion houses. Located on Via de' Tornabuoni, the street that's Florence's luxury shopping artery, this store offers some of the finest leather goods and footwear in the world. Ferragamo is known for its meticulous craftsmanship and innovation in design.

If you're a fan of classic, yet contemporary style, Ferragamo's signature shoes, especially the iconic Vara pumps, should be on your list. The store also carries a variety of leather handbags and accessories, all crafted with the highest attention to detail.

Personal Experience: During my visit, I tried on a pair of their famous shoes. The comfort was unreal—designed not only for elegance but also for wearability. Whether you're buying for yourself or searching for a thoughtful gift, Ferragamo's creations are timeless and incredibly well-made.

Insider Tip: Ferragamo offers personalized items, from monogramming leather goods to custom-made shoes. Don't hesitate to ask for this exclusive service.

3. Roberto Cavalli

Address: Via della Vigna Nuova, 40, 50123 Florence, Italy
Price Range: Dresses starting at €1,000, jackets from €1,200, shoes from €500
What to Buy: High-fashion clothing, accessories, and statement pieces

Roberto Cavalli is known for bold, extravagant fashion, and his Florence store embodies that same sense of drama and luxury. Located on Via della Vigna Nuova, the boutique is filled with vibrant prints, luxurious fabrics, and standout designs.

If you're looking for something truly eye-catching, this is the place. Cavalli's fashion pieces feature exotic prints, intricate details, and luxurious materials that exude glamour. His handbags, shoes, and accessories are perfect for those who want to make a statement.

Insider Tip: Cavalli's boutique offers personalized consultations. If you're looking for a unique, show-stopping piece, ask the staff about their styling services.

4. Louis Vuitton
Address: Via de' Tornabuoni, 5r, 50123 Florence, Italy
Price Range: Small leather goods from €200, bags starting at €1,200, and luggage from €2,000
What to Buy: Bags, leather goods, luggage, and accessories

Louis Vuitton's Florence boutique is one of the finest in Italy, offering a full range of luxury bags, leather goods, and travel accessories. Situated on the prestigious Via de' Tornabuoni, it's impossible to miss the elegant store's offerings, which combine classic craftsmanship with cutting-edge style. Whether you're looking for a timeless LV monogrammed bag or something from one of their seasonal collections, you'll find the highest-quality leather goods here. And with Florence being a hub for art and culture, you can even find exclusive Florence-themed collections.

Insider Tip: Make sure to check out Louis Vuitton's luxury luggage collection, especially if you're looking for stylish pieces for your next adventure.

5. Bvlgari
Address: Via de' Calzaiuoli, 12r, 50122 Florence, Italy
Price Range: Jewelry starting at €500, watches from €1,500, and accessories from €200
What to Buy: Fine jewelry, watches, and accessories

Bvlgari is a name that needs no introduction. Located on the picturesque Via de' Calzaiuoli, this luxurious jewelry store is one of the most famous in Florence. Known for its bold and elegant designs, Bvlgari's pieces are perfect for those looking to add a bit of sparkle to their lives.

You'll find everything from stunning diamond necklaces to luxurious watches, all crafted with impeccable attention to detail. The store also offers a variety of accessories, such as silk scarves and leather goods, perfect for a refined touch.

Insider Tip: Bvlgari's "Serpenti" collection is iconic—if you're in the market for a statement piece, this is a must-see.

6. Prada
Address: Via de' Tornabuoni, 21r, 50123 Florence, Italy
Price Range: Bags starting at €1,000, shoes from €500, and clothing from €800
What to Buy: Shoes, bags, clothing, and accessories

Prada's boutique in Florence is a mecca for high-end fashion lovers. Known for its minimalist yet bold designs, Prada brings a modern touch to classic Italian fashion. Whether you're shopping for shoes, bags, or elegant pieces of clothing, you'll find something that fits the brand's signature style of contemporary luxury.

Personal Experience: I once bought a pair of Prada boots at this very store. Not only did they fit perfectly, but the craftsmanship made them worth every penny. The sleek, modern look is versatile, making them great for both casual and formal occasions.

Insider Tip: Check out the store's exclusive seasonal collections. Some of the most sought-after items are limited-edition pieces that you won't find in other cities.

7. Emilio Pucci
Address: Via della Vigna Nuova, 9, 50123 Florence, Italy
Price Range: Dresses starting at €800, scarves from €200, and accessories from €300
What to Buy: Clothing, scarves, and accessories

Emilio Pucci's boutique is a vibrant, colorful tribute to the brand's iconic patterns and timeless style. If you're after something that's both luxurious and a little playful, Pucci's store in Florence should be on your radar. Known for its bold prints, the shop offers everything from luxurious dresses and scarves to fun accessories.

Whether you're in the mood for something casual or a dressy ensemble for a night out, Pucci's eclectic designs offer something for every occasion. The store's vibrant colors make it one of the most visually striking places to shop in Florence.

Insider Tip: Don't leave without grabbing one of Pucci's iconic printed scarves. They make for the perfect souvenir that is both stylish and practical.

Shopping Streets and Hidden Markets

Whether you're looking for leather goods, vintage items, or simply a souvenir to remember your trip, Florence offers a diverse shopping experience that blends tradition with modern style. Let's dive into some of the most popular shopping streets and hidden markets you shouldn't miss.

1. Via de' Tornabuoni

If you're looking to splurge on something special, **Via de' Tornabuoni** is where you'll find luxury shopping at its finest. This elegant street is lined with high-end boutiques from the likes of Gucci, Prada, and Ferragamo—Florence's native luxury brands. What makes this shopping experience so unique is the historical context; the street itself is a work of art, with beautiful Renaissance palaces that house these designer shops.

Address: Via de' Tornabuoni, 50123 Florence, Italy
Price Range: Luxury items ranging from €200 to over €2,000, depending on the brand.

While you're strolling down this street, don't miss the chance to visit the **Gucci Garden** at Piazza della Signoria. It's a combination of museum, shop, and café where the fashion house celebrates its rich history. For those with a taste for luxury, this street is Florence's answer to Rodeo Drive.

2. San Lorenzo Market

The **San Lorenzo Market** is an absolute must-visit for anyone who wants to experience the hustle and bustle of Florentine shopping. You'll find an overwhelming selection of leather goods, scarves, jewelry, and other artisan crafts. Most items here are handmade and represent the essence of Florence's artisanal culture. One of the things I love most about this market is that it's so vibrant and lively. The vendors are friendly, and they'll often give you a good deal if you're willing to haggle a little.

A personal favorite of mine is **Lorenzo's Leather Shop**, a small family-owned stall that sells high-quality leather jackets and bags. When I visited, the leather was soft and well-priced, and I ended up buying a classic leather belt as a souvenir that still looks great today!
Address: Piazza San Lorenzo, 50123 Florence, Italy
Price Range: Leather bags start around €30, and jackets range from €150 to €400.

3. Mercato Centrale
Although the **Mercato Centrale** is more well-known for its food offerings, it's also an excellent place to shop for local products. On the first floor, you'll find a vast selection of artisanal foods, including cheeses, wines, olive oils, and dried meats. If you're after an authentic taste of Tuscany to take home, this is the place to shop.
I particularly recommend picking up some **Tuscano Pecorino cheese** or a bottle of **Chianti Classico**. Both are quintessentially Tuscan and make great gifts or additions to your picnic basket. The prices are reasonable, and you can get a good selection of products for under €50.
Address: Piazza del Mercato Centrale, 50123 Florence, Italy
Price Range: Fresh produce and snacks can range from €5 to €50, depending on your selection.

4. Via dei Calzaiuoli
For those who want a little bit of everything, **Via dei Calzaiuoli** is the perfect spot. This bustling pedestrian street connects Piazza del Duomo with Piazza della Signoria and is home to a mix of fashion boutiques, shoe stores, and even some department stores. One of the best things about this street is that it combines the convenience of chain stores with the charm of local Florentine shops. You'll find something for every budget here.
A hidden gem on this street is **Caffè Gilli**, an old-world café where you can grab a coffee and enjoy the beautiful interior while you rest between shopping trips. Whether you're in the mood for a new pair of shoes or a trendy dress, this street has it all.

Address: Via dei Calzaiuoli, 50122 Florence, Italy
Price Range: Items here range from €15 for a scarf to €200 for a designer pair of shoes.

5. Via Santo Spirito

For a more bohemian experience, head over to **Via Santo Spirito**, located in the Oltrarno district. This area is known for its artisan workshops, vintage boutiques, and independent stores. It's where you'll find some of the most unique, handmade goods in Florence. Many of the shops specialize in **handcrafted jewelry, bespoke leather accessories, and locally designed fashion**.

One shop I highly recommend is **Ottica Tosini**, where you can pick up unique, vintage eyeglasses—perfect for anyone who loves fashion with a bit of personality. I personally found a pair of retro sunglasses that became my favorite accessory during my trip.

Address: Via Santo Spirito, 50125 Florence, Italy
Price Range: Vintage items and unique accessories range from €20 to €200.

6. Mercato di Sant'Ambrogio

The **Mercato di Sant'Ambrogio** is a lesser-known market compared to San Lorenzo, but it's a favorite among locals. Here you can buy fresh produce, local meats, and cheeses, along with handmade goods like pottery and artisan soaps. I love visiting this market for its local flavor and the chance to shop like a Florentine. It's a more relaxed experience, with less of the tourist crowd that you might find in the more famous markets.

Address: Piazza Ghiberti, 50122 Florence, Italy
Price Range: Fresh produce, cheeses, and local goods range from €5 to €50.

7. Via del Parione

For a quieter, more intimate shopping experience, **Via del Parione** is a charming little street that's perfect for boutique shopping. It's nestled near the Ponte Vecchio, so it's easy to miss, but it offers some of the best high-

end Italian fashion shops, including those selling artisan scarves, shoes, and custom-tailored clothing.
One of the shops to check out is **Raspini**, known for their collection of handmade jewelry. It's a place where you'll find one-of-a-kind pieces that you can't get anywhere else, making it perfect for someone who's looking for a special souvenir or gift.
Address: Via del Parione, 50123 Florence, Italy
Price Range: Items range from €50 for small accessories to over €500 for exclusive jewelry.

Practical Shopping Tips for Florence

Whether you're hunting for luxurious leather goods, artisan treasures, or quirky souvenirs, the city offers a wealth of shopping options. But navigating the vibrant shopping scene can be a little overwhelming for first-time visitors. Here are some practical shopping tips and real-life recommendations to make your Florence shopping experience enjoyable and worthwhile.

1. Leather Goods:

Florence is world-famous for its leather craftsmanship, and for good reason. The city has a long history of creating high-quality leather goods, from handbags to jackets to shoes. One of the best places to find top-quality leather items is the **San Lorenzo Market** (Piazza San Lorenzo). You'll find a vast array of leather vendors offering everything from stylish handbags to hand-stitched belts.

- **Tip**: Don't be swayed by the first price you hear. Leather goods in Florence often have a bit of wiggle room, so don't be afraid to haggle. For example, a leather wallet might cost anywhere from €25 to €50, but you could negotiate a better deal if you're patient.
- **Example: The Leather School (Scuola del Cuoio)** at the **Basilica di Santa Croce** (Piazza Santa Croce, 16). This famous school and

workshop sell premium leather products, including bags, wallets, and journals, often hand-stitched by artisans. A leather bag here can range from €100 to €500 depending on size and quality, and you're not just buying a bag; you're taking home a piece of Florentine tradition.

2. Handmade Jewelry and Gold

Florence is also renowned for its fine goldsmithing, especially in the historic Ponte Vecchio district. While the bridge itself is home to many jewelers, **Ceo Jewelry** (Ponte Vecchio, 16) stands out for its incredible craftsmanship and modern yet timeless designs. Whether you're looking for a souvenir or an investment piece, Ponte Vecchio is where you'll find stunning gold jewelry that's handcrafted by the city's best artisans.

- **Tip**: Florence has some of the best gold prices in Europe, so if you're interested in investing in a high-quality piece of jewelry, now's your chance. Be sure to ask about the purity of the gold (typically 18k), and always request a certificate of authenticity.

- **Example**: A pair of gold earrings or a delicate bracelet here will usually start at around €150 to €200. But, if you're looking for something special, custom-made pieces are available, and you'll find that the experience of having something created just for you adds a unique touch to your trip.

3. Fashion Boutiques for Florentine Style

Florence is home to some of Italy's most prestigious fashion houses, and the **Via de' Tornabuoni** is the city's high-end shopping street. Here, you'll find boutiques from renowned designers like Gucci, Prada, and Salvatore Ferragamo. However, the real treat is exploring the smaller, independent boutiques tucked away in the charming alleys.

- **Tip**: For a blend of classic and contemporary styles, head to **Luisa Via Roma** (Piazza Santa Trinita, 1), a high-end boutique that features cutting-edge designers and Italian luxury. While you may not be buying a designer dress on a budget, it's a great place for window shopping or picking up a trendy accessory.

- **Example**: Expect to pay €300 or more for a luxury handbag or pair of shoes in the designer stores. But smaller boutiques offer excellent quality at lower prices, with items like a silk scarf or stylish jacket ranging from €50 to €200.

4. Artisan and Vintage Markets for Unique Finds

If you prefer a more laid-back shopping experience, Florence's **Mercato delle Pulci** (Piazza dei Ciompi) is the place to be. This flea market offers an eclectic mix of antiques, vintage clothing, old books, and quirky finds. It's ideal for discovering something truly unique, whether it's an antique painting or an old leather-bound journal.

- **Tip**: While many of the items here are reasonably priced, be prepared to spend a little extra time searching for hidden gems. You can often find great bargains on vintage jewelry and old Florentine maps for around €30 to €100.

- **Example**: If you're looking for something special, try picking up a vintage leather jacket for €100 or less, or a handmade ceramic plate for about €25. There's also a selection of antique prints and postcards that make for great souvenirs.

5. Tuscan Ceramics:

One of the most delightful souvenirs you can bring back from Florence is a piece of Tuscan ceramic pottery. The shops in **Borgo San Frediano** are filled with colorful ceramics, from hand-painted plates to flowerpots and decorative tiles. **Ceramiche d'Arte** (Borgo San Frediano, 58) is a well-loved shop offering beautiful handcrafted pieces, with prices ranging from €15 for small items like cups or mugs to over €100 for larger decorative pieces.

- **Tip**: These pieces are often delicate, so make sure to pack them carefully for travel. Many shops offer to ship items back home for you, which can save you the hassle of carrying them around.
- **Example**: A hand-painted ceramic plate will cost around €30 to €50, while larger items, like a decorative vase, might run upwards of €100.

6. Art Supplies and Paper Goods

Florence is an artist's haven, and for those with a creative flair, the city's shops offer a wonderful selection of art supplies and high-quality stationery. One standout is **Zecchi Art Supplies** (Via dei Servi, 30r), where artists from all over the world buy their materials.

- **Tip**: Florence is the perfect place to pick up high-end watercolors, sketchbooks, and brushes. A quality watercolor palette might cost around €30 to €60, while a handmade sketchbook will range from €15 to €50.
- **Example**: Many visitors love purchasing unique Florentine paper, whether it's decorative or for journaling. Handcrafted journals at **Zecchi** start at €25 and make fantastic gifts or keepsakes.

7. Florentine Perfumes

For something truly distinctive, Florence offers a selection of artisanal perfumes that carry the scent of the city. **Officina Profumo-Farmaceutica di Santa Maria Novella** (Piazza Santa Maria Novella, 16), one of the oldest pharmacies in Europe, is the perfect place to experience Florentine scents.

- **Tip**: Be sure to test a few fragrances before purchasing. These perfumes are a blend of history and luxury, and a bottle will set you back anywhere from €50 to €150, depending on the scent and bottle size.

- **Example**: A classic scent like "Acqua di Colonia" starts around €60, while more elaborate fragrances or vintage collections can be priced much higher.

Outdoor Activities and Nature Escapes

Exploring the Boboli and Bardini Gardens

Nestled behind some of Florence's most iconic landmarks, these green oases offer a delightful blend of beauty, history, and panoramic views of the city. Whether you're a nature lover, an art enthusiast, or simply seeking a quiet escape, the Boboli and Bardini Gardens provide an unforgettable experience.

Boboli Gardens:
The Boboli Gardens (Giardino di Boboli) are perhaps Florence's most famous gardens, and for good reason. Located behind the Pitti Palace, this expansive garden was once the private grounds of the Medici family, who transformed it into a stunning example of Renaissance garden design. The layout of the gardens is meant to symbolize the idealized harmony between nature and humanity—a reflection of the Medici's power and wealth during the 16th century.

Why Visit?
Beyond its aesthetic beauty, Boboli Gardens offers a unique opportunity to experience a piece of history. As you stroll through the formal paths, past fountains, sculptures, and grottos, you can almost hear the echoes of Medici court life. The gardens also feature impressive sculptures from the 16th to 18th centuries, including works by Giovanni Bologna and Jean-Baptiste Carpeaux.

Real-Life Experience
I visited Boboli on a warm spring afternoon, and the gardens felt like an oasis after spending the morning wandering Florence's crowded streets. The layout is designed so that each section of the garden feels like a world

of its own. I particularly loved the Amphitheater, a circular space designed for celebrations, where I was able to sit on the steps and take in the serene beauty. The views of Florence, with the Duomo peeking over the rooftops, were breathtaking.

Address and Practical Information
- **Address:** Piazza Pitti, 1, 50125 Firenze FI, Italy
- **Opening Hours:** Daily from 8:15 AM to 6:30 PM (hours vary seasonally)
- **Entry Fee:** €10 for adults (reduced rates available for students and groups)
- **Activities:** Explore walking trails, admire sculptures, visit the Grotta del Buontalenti (a grotto with beautiful frescoes), and take in panoramic views of Florence.

Bardini Gardens: A Hidden Gem
While the Boboli Gardens attract most of the attention, the Bardini Gardens (Giardino Bardini) are often considered one of Florence's best-kept secrets. Situated just a short walk from Boboli, Bardini Gardens offer a more intimate and slightly less crowded experience. The Bardini Gardens are known for their lush greenery, terraced landscapes, and stunning views over Florence.

Why Visit?
Bardini Gardens may be smaller than Boboli, but they're just as charming. With its well-maintained hedges, winding paths, and spectacular vantage points, the gardens provide a peaceful refuge from the more tourist-heavy areas of Florence. One of the highlights of Bardini is its panoramic terrace, where visitors can enjoy sweeping views of the city, the Arno River, and the hills surrounding Florence.

Real-Life Experience
I stumbled upon Bardini Gardens while wandering through the city and, to be honest, I wasn't sure what to expect. As soon as I entered, I was struck by how quiet it was compared to other attractions in Florence. The narrow

paths led me past centuries-old trees, ivy-clad walls, and hidden nooks, each offering a sense of calm and seclusion. The view from the terrace, especially at sunset, was nothing short of magical. I stood there for a while, watching the golden light reflect off the Arno River, feeling as though I'd discovered a secret treasure in the city.

Address and Practical Information
- **Address:** Costa San Giorgio, 2, 50125 Firenze FI, Italy
- **Opening Hours:** Daily from 10:00 AM to 6:00 PM (check for seasonal changes)
- **Entry Fee:** €10 for adults
- **Activities:** Wander the beautiful gardens, enjoy views of Florence, visit the restored fountain, and take a quiet moment to appreciate the serene atmosphere.

Combining Both Gardens:
What makes visiting both Boboli and Bardini Gardens so special is that they are located within walking distance of each other, allowing you to explore two very different yet complementary gardens in one day. You can start at Boboli and work your way to Bardini, or vice versa, depending on your preference. The path connecting the two gardens is beautifully scenic and adds an extra layer of charm to your visit.

Practical Tips for Visiting
- **Plan your time wisely**: Both gardens are large, so be sure to set aside at least 2-3 hours for each one to fully immerse yourself in the experience.
- **Wear comfortable shoes**: There are a lot of hills and uneven pathways, so bring your best walking shoes.
- **Take a break**: Both gardens have cafes where you can relax with a drink while soaking in the surroundings.
- **Bring a camera**: The views are stunning, so make sure you have a camera or smartphone ready to capture the beauty.

Why You Should Visit
Florence is known for its art and history, but the Boboli and Bardini Gardens show you another side of the city—one of tranquility, nature, and unparalleled views. Whether you're a seasoned traveler looking for a quiet place to reflect or a first-time visitor hoping to escape the crowds, these gardens offer a unique perspective of Florence that few other attractions can match. So, the next time you find yourself in the city, take some time to explore these green treasures—you won't regret it.

Walking and Hiking Trails near Florence

Whether you're looking for a peaceful stroll along the Arno River or a more adventurous hike through the Tuscan hills, there's something for everyone. Here's a closer look at some of the best walking and hiking trails near Florence, each offering stunning views and an escape into the heart of nature.

1. Fiesole: The Perfect Half-Day Escape

Just a short bus ride from central Florence (about 8 km away), Fiesole is a charming hilltop town that offers one of the most scenic walks around Florence. Fiesole's **Caminetto Trail** is a popular route that begins at the town's main square and ascends into the hills above, offering breathtaking views of Florence below.
Address: Fiesole, 50014 Florence, Italy
Activities: Hiking, Photography, History
The walk to Fiesole is about a 1.5-hour journey through olive groves, cypress trees, and lush landscapes. Along the way, you'll pass the Roman Theatre, which dates back to the 1st century BCE, and the Convent of San Francesco, which provides a serene spot to take in the views. Once at the top, enjoy panoramic views of the city and the surrounding Tuscan countryside. It's a wonderful place to catch your breath and appreciate the Tuscan landscape.
Why visit? If you want to see Florence from a different perspective, this is the trail for you. The peaceful atmosphere of Fiesole makes it a great way

to escape the hustle and bustle of the city, all while enjoying some history and nature.

2. The Via degli Dei (The Way of the Gods)
For more seasoned hikers, the **Via degli Dei** is an exceptional trail that connects Florence to Bologna, covering 130 km through some of Tuscany and Emilia-Romagna's most beautiful and diverse landscapes. While the whole route can take about 5-7 days, many people opt to do shorter segments, and it's possible to take a day trip along certain stretches.
Address: Via degli Dei, Florence, Italy
Activities: Hiking, Photography, Nature Walks
The Via degli Dei takes hikers through the Apennine Mountains, past medieval villages, and through ancient forests, offering stunning views of hills, valleys, and distant mountains. You'll pass through places like the **Monte Adone**, a peak known for its panoramic views, and the **Cavone Pass**, a historic trail used by the Romans. For those based in Florence, it's easy to access the first section of the trail, which begins in **Pian del Mugnone**, located about 13 km from Florence's city center.
Why visit? This is a must-do for serious hikers looking for a multi-day trek. The diversity of landscapes and the historic significance of the trail add layers of charm and adventure. Plus, it's a fantastic way to explore the Italian countryside up close.

3. The Boboli Gardens and Surrounding Trails
Located right in the heart of Florence, the **Boboli Gardens** offers a mix of easy walking paths and more adventurous hiking opportunities, all set within a beautiful, historical setting. The gardens, which are part of the **Pitti Palace**, have been designed in the style of an Italian Renaissance garden, featuring sculptures, fountains, and groves of trees.
Address: Piazza Pitti, 1, 50125 Florence, Italy
Opening Hours: 8:15 AM – 6:30 PM (timing may vary)
While Boboli Gardens itself is an easy stroll with some gentle inclines, the surrounding areas offer trails that lead you to higher points, including **Michelangelo Hill**. The view from here is arguably one of the best

panoramas of Florence, with a sweeping view of the entire city, the Arno River, and the hills beyond.
Why visit? The Boboli Gardens offer a combination of leisurely walks and stunning views, perfect for a day when you don't want to leave the city, but still crave some nature. The gardens are also rich in history, with sculptures dating back to the 16th century.

4. Trekking in the Chianti Region
A little further out from Florence lies the **Chianti Region**, known worldwide for its vineyards and rolling hills. The area offers countless walking and hiking trails for all levels, with routes through vineyards, olive groves, and quiet rural villages. The **Chianti Classico Trail** is a particularly scenic route that winds through some of the best-known vineyards in the region.
Address: Chianti Region, Tuscany, Italy
Activities: Hiking, Wine Tasting, Photography
The **Chianti Trail** offers a 50-kilometer walk over several days, though it's easy to enjoy shorter sections that pass through charming towns like **Greve in Chianti** and **Panzano**. Along the way, stop at family-run wineries for a glass of Chianti Classico and learn about the local winemaking process.
Why visit? If you're a wine lover or simply want to experience the idyllic Tuscan countryside, this is the trail for you. The gentle hills are perfect for a relaxing hike, and stopping in a vineyard for a wine tasting is the ultimate reward at the end of the day.

5. The Arno River Walk
For those looking for a more relaxed stroll that still offers stunning views of Florence, walking along the **Arno River** is a fantastic option. You can follow the river from **Ponte Vecchio**, one of Florence's most iconic landmarks, all the way to the outskirts of the city.
Address: Arno River, Florence, Italy
Activities: Walking, Sightseeing, Photography
This easy, flat walk is perfect for those looking to enjoy the beauty of Florence from a different angle. The riverside offers scenic views of the city's historic bridges and the hills that frame it. In the early morning or late afternoon, the golden light reflecting off the river creates a magical atmosphere.

Why visit? The Arno River walk allows you to soak in Florence's beauty without the crowds of tourists. It's a peaceful way to enjoy the city and take in some of the best riverside views Florence has to offer.

Biking Along the Arno River

The Arno winds its way through Florence, offering some of the best views of the city's landmarks, as well as the quieter, hidden spots that you may otherwise overlook. Whether you're an experienced cyclist or a casual rider, biking along the Arno is one of the most enjoyable ways to experience the beauty of Florence.

Why You Should Visit

Cycling along the Arno River allows you to take in breathtaking views while exploring Florence's charming riverside. The river itself has played a central role in Florence's history, with many of the city's most iconic landmarks positioned along its banks. From the grandeur of the Ponte Vecchio to the peaceful tranquility of the Cascine Park, cycling along the Arno lets you experience the city from a different perspective—free from the crowds and at your own pace.

One of the key attractions is the **Ponte Vecchio**, Florence's most famous bridge. Pedaling along the river, you can see the bridge from a unique angle, with the colorful shops perched above the flowing waters. It's a perfect spot to pause, snap a few photos, and appreciate Florence's artistic heritage in a fresh light.

Another reason to bike along the Arno is the opportunity to explore **Cascine Park**. This lush, expansive green space, located on the western side of the river, offers plenty of shaded trails perfect for a leisurely bike ride. Cascine is Florence's largest public park, and it's where both locals and visitors come to escape the city's hustle and bustle. With wide open fields, tree-lined avenues, and peaceful paths, it's the perfect place to enjoy a relaxing bike ride while taking in the views.

Activities and What to Expect
Biking along the Arno is a flexible experience that caters to both casual riders and those looking for a more active adventure. The best part? You can customize your ride depending on your mood or schedule.

Start your journey at the **Piazza della Signoria**, right in the heart of the historic center of Florence. From here, you can head toward the riverbank and pedal along the **lungarno** (the road that runs along the river). This scenic route takes you past many of Florence's most famous attractions, including the **Uffizi Gallery** and the **Palazzo Vecchio**, with the river shimmering beside you. The road is mostly flat, making it an easy and pleasant route to follow.

A highlight of biking along the Arno is crossing the **Ponte Santa Trinita**, which offers one of the most stunning views of the Florence skyline. This bridge is known for its elegant, symmetrical design and is a favorite spot for photographers. As you cycle over, you'll be greeted with a perfect view of the Arno, the bridges, and the iconic **Duomo** in the distance.

For those who prefer a quieter, more nature-filled ride, take a detour along the southern bank of the Arno to reach **Cascine Park**. The park is a beautiful space with plenty of shaded paths, open meadows, and scenic viewpoints that overlook the river. On a sunny day, it's a great spot to slow down, enjoy a picnic, or simply watch the world go by. Locals often use this park for jogging, cycling, and even picnicking, so it's a true gem away from the main tourist trails.

Real-Life Example
During my recent trip to Florence, I rented a bike from **Tuscany Bike Tours** (located near **Piazza del Duomo**, Via Ghibellina, 88r). I started my ride in the early morning when the streets were still calm, and the sun was just beginning to rise over the Arno. The feeling of biking by the river with the soft golden light illuminating the buildings was absolutely magical. I paused near the **Ponte Santa Trinita** to take in the view and ended up chatting with a local couple who were also cycling that morning. They shared their

favorite spots in the city and recommended a small café along the river to stop for a coffee. That little interaction made the experience even more memorable.

Practical Advice
1. **Where to Rent Bikes**: There are several places to rent bikes in Florence. **Tuscany Bike Tours** is a great option for those who prefer guided tours, but there are also smaller rental shops throughout the city. Most bike rentals cost around €20-€30 for a half-day rental, which is plenty of time to enjoy the river route.
2. **Best Time to Go**: The best time for biking along the Arno is in the morning or late afternoon when the weather is cooler and the streets are less crowded. Avoid peak summer midday hours when the heat can make cycling less enjoyable.
3. **What to Wear**: Florence's cobbled streets can be tricky for cyclists, so wear comfortable shoes and clothing. If you're planning to stop and explore, pack a light jacket or sweater, as the weather can change unexpectedly, especially near the river in the evenings.
4. **Guided Tours**: If you're not familiar with Florence or would like to learn more about its history, consider joining a guided bike tour. Many tours will take you along the Arno River while sharing insights about the city's landmarks and hidden spots.
5. **Safety Tips**: Florence is generally a bike-friendly city, but always be cautious when riding near traffic. Stick to bike lanes and be mindful of pedestrians. Helmets are not mandatory, but it's a good idea to wear one if you're not used to cycling in a city environment.

Scenic Day Trips to Tuscany's Countryside

Just a short drive or train ride from Florence, the Tuscan countryside offers an unforgettable escape from the city's bustling streets. Whether you're a wine enthusiast, history lover, or nature seeker, a day trip to Tuscany is sure to delight. Here's a guide to some of the best scenic day trips you can take, complete with personal tips and advice.

1. Chianti Region:

If you've ever dreamed of wandering through endless vineyards, sipping world-class wines, and tasting fresh olive oil straight from the source, the Chianti region is for you. Located between Florence and Siena, Chianti is famous for its rolling vineyards, charming hilltop towns, and picturesque landscapes.

One of the best ways to experience Chianti is by visiting a traditional winery, or *cantina*, where you can tour the vineyard, learn about the winemaking process, and enjoy a wine tasting. Many wineries also offer local food pairings, with some even hosting cooking classes or lunch on-site.

Where to Go:

- **Castello di Verrazzano** (Address: Via Citille, 32, 50022 Greve in Chianti)
  This historic winery offers guided tours of the castle and its cellars, followed by a tasting of their famous Chianti Classico wines. The views from the castle are breathtaking and provide a perfect backdrop for a relaxed afternoon.

Why Visit: If you're looking for a genuine taste of Tuscany, the Chianti region offers a mix of tradition and scenic beauty. The wine is exceptional, the towns are charming, and you get to experience Tuscany in its most authentic form.

Personal Tip: Plan your visit in the late morning, so you can enjoy a leisurely wine tasting followed by lunch. A stop in **Greve in Chianti** is a perfect way to end your day, with its charming main square and a range of shops selling local products.

2. San Gimignano:

Known as the "Town of Fine Towers," San Gimignano is a UNESCO World Heritage Site famous for its medieval architecture and stunning views over the surrounding countryside. The town is perched on a hill, and its skyline is dominated by 14 well-preserved towers that date back to the Middle Ages.

A visit to San Gimignano feels like stepping back in time, with cobblestone streets, charming piazzas, and artisan shops. The town is also famous for its saffron and gelato, making it a great place to indulge in local specialties.

Where to Go:

- **Piazza del Duomo**: The heart of San Gimignano, surrounded by historic buildings and towering churches. Don't miss the **Collegiate Church of Santa Maria Assunta**, known for its frescoes and historical significance.

Why Visit: San Gimignano offers a rare glimpse into Tuscany's medieval past. It's small enough to explore in a few hours but packed with history and beauty.

Personal Tip: After walking through the town, stop for a gelato at **Gelateria Dondoli** (Piazza della Cisterna, 4). This award-winning gelateria is famous for its creative flavors, such as saffron and raspberry.

3. Cortona:

Cortona, made famous by the book and film *Under the Tuscan Sun*, is another gem in Tuscany's countryside. This charming town offers stunning views over the Val di Chiana, with narrow streets, stone buildings, and a warm, welcoming atmosphere. While Cortona may be quieter than some of Tuscany's bigger cities, it is no less captivating.

Where to Go:

- **Piazza della Repubblica**: This bustling square is the heart of the town, surrounded by cafes, restaurants, and shops.

- **Eremo Le Celle**: A peaceful Franciscan hermitage located just outside the town, offering a serene escape and panoramic views.

Why Visit: Cortona offers a perfect blend of history, art, and nature. It's smaller than Florence, but it still offers plenty to explore, from ancient Etruscan ruins to art galleries and local markets.

Personal Tip: Make sure to take a walk around the town's medieval walls for some of the best views of the surrounding countryside. If you're a fan of the *Under the Tuscan Sun* film, visit **Villa Laura**, the villa where Frances (Diane Lane) stays in the movie.

4. Val d'Orcia: A UNESCO-Listed Landscape

For those looking to truly immerse themselves in Tuscany's breathtaking natural beauty, a trip to **Val d'Orcia** is a must. This region is known for its striking landscapes, complete with cypress trees, rolling hills, and golden fields. Val d'Orcia is often featured in postcard images of Tuscany, and for good reason—it's stunning.

Where to Go:

- **Pienza** (Address: Piazza Pio II, 53026 Pienza): A Renaissance town with narrow streets and picturesque squares. The town is famous for its Pecorino cheese and offers incredible views over the Val d'Orcia valley.

- **Bagno Vignoni**: A unique town with an ancient thermal pool at its center. The town has been a wellness retreat for centuries, offering a relaxing escape in the midst of the countryside.

Why Visit: Val d'Orcia offers the quintessential Tuscan landscape—perfect for photography, hiking, or simply relaxing. The towns here are beautiful and often less crowded than Florence or Siena.

Personal Tip: Make sure to stop at a local agriturismo for a lunch featuring locally produced olive oil, cheese, and wine. You'll be amazed by the flavors and the warm hospitality.

5. Siena:
Though Siena is technically a city, it feels like a small, picturesque town. Located about an hour south of Florence, Siena is famed for its medieval architecture, narrow streets, and the iconic **Piazza del Campo**, one of the most beautiful squares in Italy.

Where to Go:

- **Piazza del Campo**: Known for the famous Palio horse race, this square is the heart of Siena's social life.

- **Duomo di Siena**: A beautiful Gothic cathedral with intricate mosaics and marble floors.

Why Visit: Siena offers a deep dive into Italy's medieval past, with its rich art, architecture, and history. The city has a peaceful, relaxed vibe, making it a perfect day trip from Florence.

Personal Tip: Try the local delicacy, **panforte**, a spiced fruitcake that's popular during the holidays but available year-round in many bakeries.

Hot Air Ballooning and Vineyard Visits

While exploring the city's museums and historic buildings is a must, there's something truly magical about experiencing the beauty of the region from above—through hot air ballooning—and pairing it with a visit to one of the world's most famous wine regions. Let's dive into how these two unforgettable experiences can make your Florence trip even more special.

Hot Air Ballooning Over Tuscany:
Imagine floating high above the rolling hills, vineyards, and olive groves of Tuscany. The experience of hot air ballooning here is serene, yet thrilling, offering a unique way to take in the stunning landscapes. Hot air ballooning is one of those activities that combine adventure with tranquility, offering

panoramic views of the medieval villages, patchwork farms, and the famous Chianti hills that surround Florence.

A popular provider for this experience is **Tuscany Ballooning**, which offers daily flights, weather permitting, over the Tuscan countryside. Their launch sites are located just a short drive from Florence, often in the hills near **San Casciano Val di Pesa**, about 30 minutes from the city center. The beauty of hot air ballooning is that the experience is highly weather-dependent, so each flight offers a new view, depending on the wind and the time of day.

Flight Details:
- **Location**: San Casciano Val di Pesa (or nearby areas)
- **Duration**: Around 1 hour in the air, plus pre-flight preparations
- **Cost**: Approximately €250-€300 per person
- **When**: Flights are offered at sunrise, when the weather is most calm, and sometimes at sunset, providing different lighting and unique perspectives of the landscape.

Why You Should Try It:

The moment you lift off from the ground, it feels as if time slows down. The gentle breeze, the quiet hum of the burner, and the ever-changing landscape below create an almost surreal experience. As you float higher, Florence, with its iconic red rooftops and the Duomo's dome, appears in the distance, set against a backdrop of lush hills and cypress trees. The Tuscan vineyards and olive groves below look like patchwork quilts—each field a different shade of green.

One of the best aspects of hot air ballooning is the sense of freedom it provides. There's no noise, no rush—just a calm and peaceful ride over one of the most beautiful regions in the world. And at the end of the flight, many ballooning companies offer a celebratory glass of champagne to toast your experience.

Vineyard Visits:

After you've soared through the sky, why not descend to the rolling hills for a visit to a vineyard? Tuscany is synonymous with world-class wine, particularly Chianti, and its vineyards offer a chance to taste some of the finest wines while immersing yourself in the landscape that produced them.

A popular stop is **Castello di Verrazzano**, located in the heart of the Chianti Classico region, just a short drive from the ballooning area. This historic winery is set on a hill with sweeping views of the vineyards and surrounding countryside. The castle itself dates back to the 14th century, and visitors can tour the vineyards, wine cellars, and enjoy wine tastings.

Vineyard Tour Details:
- **Location**: Castello di Verrazzano, Greve in Chianti
- **Activities**: Vineyard and cellar tours, wine tastings, gourmet lunch options
- **Cost**: Tours range from €25-€50 per person, depending on the experience (basic tour to full lunch with wine pairings)
- **When**: Open year-round, with special events during the harvest season (September and October)
- **Address**: Via Citille, 32, 50022 Greve in Chianti, Florence, Italy

Why You Should Visit:
A visit to a Tuscan vineyard is more than just about tasting great wine. It's about experiencing the art and history behind the wine-making process. The experts at Castello di Verrazzano walk you through their techniques, some of which have been passed down for generations. The estate offers multiple tour options, ranging from short tastings to more comprehensive, wine-pairing experiences. One of the highlights is enjoying the wines with a traditional Tuscan meal, featuring local cheeses, meats, and bread—food that perfectly complements the rich and earthy wines of the region.

A Personal Anecdote:
During my own visit to Castello di Verrazzano, I took part in a wine-tasting

tour that included a delicious multi-course meal. We sat outside under a pergola, with the Tuscan sun casting golden light over the vineyards. The wine expert guided us through each pour, explaining the subtle flavors and the terroir of the land. One of the wines, a rich Chianti Classico, paired perfectly with the wild boar ragu. It was a moment I'll never forget—the peace of the countryside, the satisfaction of a good meal, and the connection to the land that produces such incredible wine.

Tips for Making the Most of Both Experiences
- **Book in Advance**: Both hot air ballooning and vineyard visits can be popular, especially in the high season (spring to fall). Booking in advance will ensure that you don't miss out on these experiences.
- **Dress Comfortably**: For ballooning, wear layers, as it can be chilly early in the morning but warms up quickly. Comfortable shoes are also important, as you may need to walk a short distance to the launch site. For vineyard visits, wear comfortable shoes for walking through the vineyard and cellar, and be prepared for some uneven terrain.
- **Combine Experiences**: Many hot air ballooning companies offer packaged deals that include a vineyard tour after your flight. This is a great way to combine two of Tuscany's best offerings into one unforgettable day.

Picnic Spots and Panoramic Views

Whether you're looking to escape the hustle and bustle of the city or simply soak in the beauty of its rolling hills and majestic views, Florence has several spots that invite you to sit back, relax, and enjoy a moment of tranquility.

1. Piazzale Michelangelo
Address: Piazzale Michelangelo, 50125 Florence
When you think of panoramic views of Florence, Piazzale Michelangelo is likely the first spot that comes to mind. Situated on a hill just south of the Arno River, this square offers a breathtaking vista of the city, including a

clear view of the iconic Duomo, the Ponte Vecchio, and the surrounding Tuscan hills. It's one of Florence's most famous viewpoints, and for good reason.

For an unforgettable picnic experience, grab some snacks from the nearby San Lorenzo Market or a local bakery, and make your way up to Piazzale Michelangelo. Bring a blanket, find a spot on the grass, and enjoy the view as the city's orange rooftops glow under the sun. If you're up for a bit of exercise, you can also take the 10-minute walk up from the Arno River, which will give you even more opportunities to stop and snap photos along the way.

Why You Should Visit: The panoramic view of Florence is unmatched, especially at sunset when the sky is painted in hues of pink and orange. It's the perfect spot to relax and soak in the beauty of the city. If you visit in the evening, you'll be joined by locals who come here to unwind after work, making it a great place to people-watch.

Best Time to Visit: Late afternoon and evening for the best views, especially at sunset. The early morning is also quieter for a peaceful escape.

2. Boboli Gardens (Giardino di Boboli)
Address: Piazza Pitti, 1, 50125 Florence

Boboli Gardens, located behind the grand Pitti Palace, is one of Florence's most beautiful green spaces. These gardens are a perfect blend of nature and art, with its meticulously designed landscapes, fountains, sculptures, and hidden grottos. While it's a popular spot for tourists, the gardens offer plenty of quiet, secluded areas to spread out a blanket and enjoy a peaceful picnic.

One of the most charming features of Boboli Gardens is its panoramic views of the city. From the top of the hill, you can see the entire city, with the dome of the Duomo standing proudly in the distance. It's a perfect spot to relax, enjoy a bottle of Chianti, and indulge in some Tuscan cheeses and meats, which can easily be found at local delicatessens.

Why You Should Visit: Boboli Gardens combines natural beauty with historical significance. It's a place where you can enjoy both a delightful picnic and a leisurely stroll through Italy's cultural history. As you explore, you'll stumble upon fountains, statues, and even an amphitheater that add to the garden's allure.

Best Time to Visit: Spring and fall are ideal, as the gardens are lush, and the weather is perfect for a relaxing day outside. In summer, it can get quite hot, so early morning or late afternoon is better.

3. Giardino delle Rose (Rose Garden)
Address: Viale Giuseppe Poggi, 50125 Florence
Just below Piazzale Michelangelo, the Giardino delle Rose (Rose Garden) is a hidden gem that not many tourists know about. This peaceful garden, which blooms with hundreds of different types of roses during the warmer months, offers a more intimate picnic experience. There are plenty of benches and shaded spots where you can sit and enjoy the fragrant flowers, or if you prefer, you can lay out your picnic blanket on the grassy areas overlooking the Arno River.

The view from the garden is not as grand as Piazzale Michelangelo, but it still offers a lovely perspective of Florence, with the Ponte Vecchio and Palazzo Vecchio visible in the distance. Plus, the garden's serene atmosphere, filled with the sound of birds chirping and the scent of roses, makes it a wonderful spot to escape the crowds.

Why You Should Visit: The Giardino delle Rose is a peaceful, less crowded alternative to the more famous views in Florence. If you're a nature lover or someone who enjoys the beauty of flowers, this is the place for you. It's also a great location for photography, especially when the roses are in full bloom.

Best Time to Visit: Late spring to early summer, when the roses are in bloom. However, it's lovely year-round, with a more quiet atmosphere in the off-season.

4. Cascine Park (Parco delle Cascine)

Address: Viale degli Ammiragli, 50144 Florence

If you're looking for a larger, more expansive park to enjoy a picnic in Florence, head to the Cascine Park, the city's largest public park. Situated along the Arno River, the park is a favorite among locals for running, cycling, and picnicking. The park has vast open spaces, shaded areas, and plenty of green lawns, making it an ideal spot for a relaxing picnic.

During weekends, you'll find Florentines enjoying their time here, often with a family gathering or a casual barbecue. You can pick up fresh bread, cheese, and prosciutto from the local markets and enjoy a laid-back picnic by the river. The park also has a café and an old villa, which are great for a post-picnic coffee or gelato.

Why You Should Visit: Cascine Park offers a more "local" experience compared to the tourist-heavy spots in Florence. It's an excellent place to enjoy a peaceful day outdoors, especially if you want to get away from the busy historic center.

Best Time to Visit: Spring and summer, when the weather is perfect for outdoor activities. The park is especially lively on weekends.

5. Fiesole
Address: Fiesole, 50014 Florence
For a more adventurous picnic with a stunning panoramic view, take a short trip to Fiesole, a charming hilltop town just a few miles outside of Florence. From here, you can see the entire Florence skyline, the rolling Tuscan hills, and the green valleys below. Fiesole is perfect for a picnic after exploring its ancient Roman ruins and tranquil streets.

Once you reach the top of the hill, there are several lovely spots to lay out your blanket and enjoy your meal with a view. You can pack your picnic, take the bus or drive up, and experience a quieter, more laid-back vibe compared to central Florence.

Why You Should Visit: Fiesole is a peaceful escape from the city, offering not only great panoramic views but also a chance to explore the historical ruins of a Roman theater and baths. It's a perfect spot for a full-day outing from Florence.

Best Time to Visit: Early morning or late afternoon for a peaceful experience and the best light for photos.

Tips for Enjoying Florence's Natural Beauty

Whether you're a nature lover looking to unwind in lush gardens, or someone who prefers an active day out in the hills surrounding the city, Florence has plenty to offer. Here's how to make the most of the city's green spaces and stunning outdoor scenery.

1. Take a Stroll Through the Boboli Gardens

Located just behind the Pitti Palace, the Boboli Gardens (Piazza de' Pitti, 1, 50125 Florence) are an iconic example of Renaissance landscaping. Walking through these beautifully manicured gardens, you're treated to breathtaking views of Florence, from the Duomo to the rolling Tuscan hills beyond. The garden itself is a masterpiece of design, with sculptures, fountains, and pathways that guide you through its vast 11-acre grounds.

Why visit: The Boboli Gardens are not just a great escape from the crowds, they offer an opportunity to immerse yourself in the kind of tranquil beauty that inspired some of the greatest artists and thinkers of the Renaissance.

If you enjoy photography, this place offers endless photo opportunities, from the towering cypress trees to the statues that line the long avenues.

Tip: If you want to avoid the crowds, head there early in the morning when the gardens are less busy, and you can enjoy the serenity before the heat of the day sets in.

2. Enjoy the Scenic Views from Piazzale Michelangelo

For one of the best panoramic views of Florence, you can't beat Piazzale Michelangelo. This square (Viale Michelangelo, 50125 Florence) sits on a hill just south of the Arno River, offering sweeping vistas of the city, including the iconic Duomo, Ponte Vecchio, and the hills of Tuscany in the distance. The view is especially stunning at sunrise or sunset when the city's skyline is bathed in golden light.

Why visit: If you're looking for a romantic spot or a place to take in the beauty of the city from above, Piazzale Michelangelo is the perfect choice. It's a popular spot for both tourists and locals, and there's a bronze replica of Michelangelo's David at the center, adding to the artistic vibe of the location.

Tip: If you're feeling energetic, take the walk up to Piazzale Michelangelo from the city center—it's a bit of a climb, but the views along the way make it worthwhile. Alternatively, you can take the bus or a taxi to the top if you prefer a more leisurely ascent.

3. Discover the Tranquility of the Bardini Gardens

Not far from the Boboli Gardens, the Bardini Gardens (Costa San Giorgio, 2, 50125 Florence) are another green oasis, though they tend to be quieter and less crowded. With their romantic, intimate atmosphere, these gardens feature winding paths, a charming small pond, and views over Florence that rival those of the Boboli Gardens.

Why visit: If you're looking for a more peaceful and serene spot to relax, the Bardini Gardens offer a perfect escape. The gardens are especially known for their beautiful wisteria-covered terrace in the spring, creating a spectacular sight and aroma.

Tip: Don't miss the panoramic terrace at the top of the hill—it's the perfect spot for a photo op, with sweeping views of the Arno River and Florence laid out before you.

4. Hike Up to Fiesole for Stunning Views of Florence and Tuscany

Fiesole is a small hilltop town just outside of Florence, known for its ancient Roman ruins and stunning views. From the town, you can look out over the entire Florence valley, with the Duomo and the hills of Tuscany providing a picturesque backdrop.

Why visit: Fiesole is a perfect spot for a day trip to experience the natural beauty surrounding Florence. The hike to the town offers an opportunity to get out of the city and into the Tuscan countryside, with peaceful paths that wind through olive groves and forests. At the top, you'll find a Roman theater, an archaeological museum, and, of course, plenty of places to stop for a coffee with a view.

Tip: The hike from Florence to Fiesole is about 45 minutes to an hour and is relatively easy, making it a great choice for walkers. If you prefer not to hike, there are buses that run regularly from the city center.

5. Cycle Along the Arno River

Cycling along the Arno River is a fantastic way to enjoy the natural beauty of Florence while staying active. The paths along the river offer a scenic route through the city and beyond, with plenty of spots to stop and admire the views. You can rent a bike from one of the many rental shops in the city, such as *Florence by Bike* (Via dei Cimatori, 50122 Florence).

Why visit: Biking is an excellent way to explore Florence at your own pace, and riding along the Arno lets you experience the city from a different perspective. It's also a great option for families or those who want to cover more ground while enjoying the outdoors.

Tip: The best time to bike along the river is early morning or late afternoon, when the weather is cooler and the streets are less crowded.

6. Picnic in Cascine Park

Cascine Park (Piazzale delle Cascine, 50144 Florence) is the largest public park in Florence and a beloved spot for both locals and visitors. Stretching along the Arno River, it offers expansive green spaces perfect for a relaxing picnic. The park is home to beautiful walking paths, shady areas, and even a small lake.

Why visit: Cascine Park is ideal for anyone looking to enjoy Florence's outdoor beauty without leaving the city. It's perfect for a casual day out, whether you're walking, cycling, or just lounging on the grass. It's also a great spot for families, as there are playgrounds for kids.

Tip: On Sundays, you can visit the park's weekly farmers' market, where you can pick up fresh produce, homemade goods, and local specialties to enjoy during your picnic.

7. Visit the Tuscan Vineyards

The rolling hills around Florence are home to some of Italy's most famous vineyards, including those in the Chianti region. A visit to the Tuscan vineyards is a great way to experience the natural beauty of the region while indulging in its world-class wines. Many vineyards offer tours, where you can explore the vines, learn about the winemaking process, and sample the local Chianti wines.

Why visit: A vineyard tour allows you to immerse yourself in the picturesque countryside, with breathtaking views of vineyards, olive groves, and small villages dotting the landscape. It's a peaceful and indulgent way to experience the essence of Tuscany.

Tip: Book a half-day or full-day wine tour from Florence to get the most out of your experience. There are many tours that offer transportation, making it easy to relax and enjoy the day without worrying about driving.

Suggested Itineraries

Florence in One Day:

If you've only got one day to experience Florence, it can feel like a bit of a rush, but don't worry! The city is compact, walkable, and packed with iconic sites, so it's absolutely possible to get a taste of its beauty and history. You might have to skip a few things, but with this itinerary, you'll hit the top spots and still have time to soak in the atmosphere of this Renaissance city.

Morning:
Start your day early to make the most of your time. **Piazza del Duomo** should be your first stop. This iconic square is home to Florence's most famous landmarks: the **Cathedral of Santa Maria del Fiore** (better known as the Duomo), **Giotto's Campanile**, and the **Baptistry of St. John**. The grandeur of the Duomo is awe-inspiring, and the intricate details on the façade will leave you staring for a while.

Why You Should Visit: The Duomo's dome, designed by Filippo Brunelleschi, is an architectural marvel and a must-see. Climbing to the top gives you a stunning view of the city.

Tip: If you're up for a climb, the **Duomo's Dome** (address: Piazza del Duomo, 50122 Florence) offers panoramic views of the city and beyond. The climb is 463 steps, but the reward is worth it. If you're short on time, you can admire the cathedral from the square and explore the nearby **Museo dell'Opera del Duomo**, where you'll find works by Donatello and Michelangelo.

After taking in the Duomo, take a short stroll to **Piazza della Signoria**, the political heart of Florence, just a 5-minute walk away. Here, you'll find the imposing **Palazzo Vecchio**, which served as the seat of government during the Renaissance. Right outside the Palazzo is **Loggia dei Lanzi**, an open-air gallery housing some striking sculptures, including **Perseus with the Head of Medusa** by Benvenuto Cellini.

Why You Should Visit: This piazza is like an open-air museum. The palaces and sculptures in the square give you a quick history lesson on Florence's political and artistic past.

Late Morning:
From Piazza della Signoria, head towards the **Uffizi Gallery** (address: Piazzale degli Uffizi, 6, 50122 Florence), one of the world's most famous art museums. If you're pressed for time, focus on the highlights: **Botticelli's "The Birth of Venus"**, **Leonardo da Vinci's "Annunciation"**, and **Michelangelo's "Tondo Doni"**. Even if you're not an art connoisseur, the history and beauty in these paintings will captivate you.

Why You Should Visit: Florence is the birthplace of the Renaissance, and the Uffizi is where you can witness its most famous artists and masterpieces.

Tip: To avoid long lines, it's best to book tickets in advance. The museum can be overwhelming, so if you're short on time, ask the staff for a quick guide to the must-see rooms.

Once you've had your fill of Renaissance masterpieces, head to **Ponte Vecchio**, Florence's oldest bridge, which is just a 10-minute walk from the Uffizi. Here, you'll find a row of jewelers' shops that have been there for centuries. Whether you plan to shop for a keepsake or simply take in the view of the Arno River, it's a must-visit spot for any Florence itinerary.

Why You Should Visit: Ponte Vecchio is iconic and offers one of the best photo ops in Florence, especially with the colorful buildings reflecting in the Arno.

Lunch:
After exploring the top attractions, it's time for lunch. Florence is known for its hearty, flavorful cuisine, so treat yourself to a traditional Tuscan meal. For a quick yet delicious option, head to **Osteria All'Antico Vinaio** (address: Via dei Neri, 74/R, 50122 Florence), a local favorite where you can grab a **schiacciata** (a type of flatbread sandwich filled with local meats, cheeses, and vegetables). Pair it with a glass of Tuscan wine, and you'll have a meal that's as satisfying as it is authentic.

Tip: If you're in the mood for a sit-down meal, Florence is also home to plenty of trattorias offering classics like **bistecca alla fiorentina** (Florentine steak) and **ribollita** (a hearty vegetable soup).

Afternoon:
After lunch, take a stroll across the Arno River to the **Oltrarno District**, known for its quieter, more local vibe. The area is home to artisan workshops, independent boutiques, and some of Florence's best-hidden gems. One spot worth seeking out is **Basilica di Santo Spirito** (address: Piazza Santo Spirito, 50125 Florence), a less-crowded church designed by Brunelleschi, with a peaceful atmosphere that provides a nice contrast to the tourist-heavy areas.

Why You Should Visit: The Oltrarno offers a more authentic Florence experience, where you can explore beyond the main attractions and discover the city's creative side.

Late Afternoon:
Finish off your one-day Florence adventure with a visit to **Piazzale Michelangelo** (address: Piazzale Michelangelo, 50125 Florence), a hilltop square with breathtaking panoramic views of the city. It's a bit of a hike, but if you're not up for the walk, you can take a short bus ride from the city center.
Why You Should Visit: The view from Piazzale Michelangelo is one of the most iconic in Florence. You'll see the entire city laid out before you, with the Duomo, the Ponte Vecchio, and the rolling Tuscan hills in the distance.

Tip: If you've got time, grab a gelato from a nearby stand and watch the sunset over the city for the perfect end to your whirlwind Florence day.

Florence in Two Days:

If you're short on time, a two-day itinerary focused on art and architecture is the perfect way to dive deep into what makes Florence so special. Here's how to make the most of your time in this mesmerizing city.

Day 1:
Morning: The Duomo and Santa Maria del Fiore
Start your Florence adventure with the iconic *Duomo*, officially known as *Cattedrale di Santa Maria del Fiore*. This cathedral is the centerpiece of Florence's skyline, with its stunning red-tiled dome designed by Filippo Brunelleschi. It's one of the largest churches in Europe, and the scale of the structure alone is breathtaking. To make the most of your visit, climb to the top of the dome (address: Piazza del Duomo) for panoramic views of the city. It's a bit of a hike—463 steps—but the vista is worth every step. Be sure to book your tickets online in advance to avoid long lines, especially in the peak tourist months.

Once at the top, take a moment to appreciate the Duomo's intricate frescoes, painted by Giorgio Vasari and Federico Zuccari. You'll see Florence spread out beneath you, with its terracotta rooftops, medieval towers, and modern elements. From here, head into the cathedral itself, where you can admire its stunning interior, especially the intricate mosaics that decorate the interior of the dome.

Why Visit? The Duomo is more than just a church; it's a symbol of Florence's artistic and architectural grandeur. If you're an architecture or art lover, this is a must-see.

Lunch Break:
After a morning of awe-inspiring architecture, head to a nearby trattoria for a delicious Florentine meal. Try some traditional *ribollita* (a hearty vegetable and bean soup) or *bistecca alla fiorentina* (Florentine steak) at a restaurant like *Trattoria Mario* (Address: Via Rosina, 2r).

Afternoon: Uffizi Gallery
In the afternoon, it's time to explore one of the world's greatest art collections: the *Uffizi Gallery* (Address: Piazzale degli Uffizi, 6). Home to masterpieces by Botticelli, Michelangelo, and Leonardo da Vinci, the Uffizi is a treasure trove of Renaissance art. Highlights include *The Birth of Venus* by Botticelli and *Annunciation* by Leonardo.

Make sure to take your time here—there's so much to see! If you're an art enthusiast, consider booking a guided tour to gain deeper insights into the works and the artists behind them. A professional guide can help you navigate the maze of paintings and sculptures, bringing history to life in a way that self-guided tours can't.

Why Visit? The Uffizi isn't just a museum; it's a journey through the history of Western art. For those passionate about the Renaissance, this is a sacred spot.

Evening: Ponte Vecchio
As the day winds down, head to the *Ponte Vecchio* (Address: Ponte Vecchio), one of Florence's most famous landmarks. This medieval stone bridge is lined with jewelry shops and offers picturesque views of the Arno River. The bridge has a rich history, once being home to butchers and fishmongers before the city decided to only allow goldsmiths and jewelers.
Take a stroll across, and if you're up for it, stop for an aperitivo at one of the river-facing cafes, like *Bardini Café* (Address: Costa San Giorgio, 2). Enjoy a glass of *vin santo* (a local dessert wine) while watching the sunset over Florence's rooftops.

Day 2:
Morning: Galleria dell'Accademia

Start your second day at the *Galleria dell'Accademia* (Address: Via Ricasoli, 58/60), home to Michelangelo's *David*. The statue is the epitome of Renaissance art, and seeing it in person is truly humbling. Spend some time here appreciating Michelangelo's mastery, not only in David but also in the unfinished *Prisoners*, which give you a glimpse of his working process.

While the statue of David gets the most attention, the museum also hosts other gems, like *St. Matthew* and a collection of Renaissance paintings. The Accademia is smaller than the Uffizi, making it perfect for a morning visit.

Why Visit? Michelangelo's *David* is an enduring symbol of human potential, and seeing it up close is an unforgettable experience for anyone interested in sculpture or art history.

Lunch: A Taste of Tuscany

After your visit to the Accademia, enjoy lunch at *Osteria dell'Enoteca* (Address: Via Ghibellina, 87), which serves traditional Tuscan dishes like *pappardelle* with wild boar ragu and a great selection of local wines.

Afternoon: Palazzo Vecchio and Piazza della Signoria

In the afternoon, head to *Piazza della Signoria*, the political heart of Florence, where the *Palazzo Vecchio* (Address: Piazza della Signoria) stands as a testament to the city's power. Inside, you'll find more masterpieces, including works by Donatello, and a fascinating glimpse into Florence's political past.

The *Hall of Five Hundred* is particularly spectacular, with its massive frescoes by Giorgio Vasari. Don't forget to climb the tower for another great view of Florence.

Why Visit? Palazzo Vecchio is not only an architectural marvel but also a living piece of history, reflecting Florence's significance during the Renaissance.

Evening: Sunset at Michelangelo Square

Wrap up your two-day exploration of Florence with a visit to *Piazzale Michelangelo* (Address: Viale Michelangelo), a scenic spot across the Arno River with a panoramic view of the city. It's the perfect place to reflect on the city's beauty and to capture that iconic shot of Florence's skyline with the Duomo in the foreground.

If you're not tired, consider dining at *La Loggia* (Address: Piazzale Michelangelo), where you can enjoy a delicious dinner with a view of the entire city.

Why Visit? The sunset views from Piazzale Michelangelo are unmatched, offering an unforgettable, picturesque conclusion to your Florence journey.

Florence in Three Days:

Florence, the birthplace of the Renaissance, is a city brimming with art, history, and culture at every turn. Spending three days here offers the perfect balance of exploring its most famous sites, discovering hidden gems, and soaking in the unique atmosphere that makes Florence one of the most enchanting cities in the world. Here's how you can spend three unforgettable days in Florence, immersing yourself in its full Renaissance splendor.

Day 1: The Heart of Florence

Start your journey in Florence's historic center, where nearly every street and square tells a story. Your first stop should be **Piazza del Duomo**, home to the iconic **Cathedral of Santa Maria del Fiore** (The Duomo). With its striking red dome designed by Filippo Brunelleschi, this cathedral is a masterpiece of Renaissance architecture. If you're feeling adventurous, climb the 463 steps to the top of the dome for a breathtaking panoramic view of the city (Address: Piazza del Duomo, 50122 Florence). It's a workout, but the view is worth it!

From the Duomo, head over to the **Galleria dell'Accademia** (Address: Via Ricasoli 58/60, 50122 Florence), where you'll encounter Michelangelo's famous statue of **David**. Standing 17 feet tall, this marble masterpiece embodies the peak of Renaissance art. The museum also has other works by Michelangelo, but David is the undisputed star.

Lunch could be a leisurely affair at one of the nearby cafes in the **Piazza della Signoria**, a bustling square that is home to the **Palazzo Vecchio** (Address: Piazza della Signoria, 50122 Florence). Here, you can also marvel at replicas of famous sculptures like **Perseus with the Head of Medusa** by Benvenuto Cellini. For a taste of Florence's authentic flavors, try a **panino** (sandwich) filled with **porchetta** (roast pork) from a local deli.

In the afternoon, visit the **Uffizi Gallery** (Address: Piazzale degli Uffizi, 6, 50122 Florence), which houses an unparalleled collection of Renaissance masterpieces. Among the highlights are Botticelli's **The Birth of Venus** and Leonardo da Vinci's **Annunciation**. It's best to book tickets in advance to avoid long lines—this museum is always busy! As you wander through the halls, take a moment to appreciate how these artists shaped not just Florence, but the entire world's perception of art.

In the evening, enjoy dinner at **Trattoria ZaZa** (Address: Piazza del Mercato Centrale, 50123 Florence), known for its hearty Tuscan dishes like **ribollita** (vegetable soup) and **bistecca alla fiorentina** (Florentine steak). The vibrant atmosphere here perfectly captures the spirit of Florence.

Day 2: The Oltrarno District
On your second day, cross the **Ponte Vecchio** (Address: Ponte Vecchio, 50125 Florence) to reach the **Oltrarno District**, where you'll discover a more local and less touristy side of Florence. This neighborhood is packed with artisan workshops, quaint cafes, and some of the city's most beautiful gardens.

Start your morning with a visit to the **Palazzo Pitti** (Address: Piazza de' Pitti, 1, 50125 Florence), once the residence of the powerful Medici family. The palace is home to the **Palatine Gallery** and **Royal Apartments**, but the real treasure is the **Boboli Gardens** at the back. Stroll through this expansive green space, filled with sculptures, fountains, and terraced hills that offer stunning views of Florence and the surrounding countryside. It's a peaceful escape from the crowds in the city center.

After a leisurely lunch at **Trattoria Omero** (Address: Via dei Serragli, 108, 50124 Florence), head to the **Basilica di Santo Spirito** (Address: Piazza Santo Spirito, 50125 Florence). This church, designed by Brunelleschi, is a hidden gem that many tourists miss. It's less crowded than the Duomo but equally impressive with its serene interior.

In the afternoon, take time to explore the quirky artisan shops on **Via de' Serragli** and **Via di Santo Spirito**. You'll find everything from hand-crafted leather goods to traditional Florentine paper. Stop by **Scuola del Cuoio** (Address: Piazza Santa Croce, 16, 50122 Florence), a historic leather school, where you can watch artisans at work and purchase unique leather products directly from the craftsmen.

As the sun sets, head to the **Piazza del Carmine** for a drink at **Caffè degli Artigiani** (Address: Piazza del Carmine, 50124 Florence), a cozy bar known for its innovative cocktails and local wine list.

Day 3: Day Trip to Tuscany
On your final day, take a day trip to explore the Tuscan countryside, just a short drive from Florence. If you love wine, the **Chianti Region** is a must-visit. A guided wine tour will take you through lush vineyards and charming medieval villages like **Greve in Chianti** and **Radda in Chianti**. Visit a local winery like **Castello di Verrazzano** (Address: Via Citille, 32, 50020 Greve in Chianti, Florence), where you can tour the cellars and enjoy a wine tasting with views of rolling hills dotted with vineyards.

If you prefer a more relaxed day, visit the medieval town of **San Gimignano** (about 1.5 hours from Florence). Known as the "Medieval Manhattan" because of its impressive towers, San Gimignano offers an authentic glimpse of Italy's past. Wander through its cobbled streets, visit the **Collegiate Church of Santa Maria Assunta** (Address: Piazza del Duomo, 53037 San Gimignano), and sample the town's famous **gelato** at **Gelateria Dondoli** (Address: Piazza della Cisterna, 53037 San Gimignano).

Return to Florence in the late afternoon for a relaxed evening in **Piazza della Repubblica**. Here, enjoy a gelato while people-watching, and take in the vibrancy of the city as you reflect on your journey through its rich history and culture.

A Week in Florence:

If you're lucky enough to have a full week in this stunning city, you'll have the chance to dive deep into its wonders, both famous and hidden. Here's a suggested itinerary that will guide you through a perfect week in Florence, allowing you to savor all its iconic attractions and discover the secrets that make this city so special.

Day 1: Welcome to Florence
Morning:
Start your journey with a stroll through Florence's historical center. Head straight to the **Piazza del Duomo**, home to the iconic Cathedral of Santa Maria del Fiore (the Duomo). Make your first stop at the **Duomo Museum** (Piazza del Duomo, 9), which offers insight into the cathedral's history and the masterpiece by architect Filippo Brunelleschi—the dome itself. For an incredible view of Florence, climb the 463 steps to the top of the Duomo, or opt for the easier elevator ride to the top of the **Giotto's Campanile** (bell tower) right next door.

Afternoon:
For lunch, wander through the **Piazza della Signoria**, the city's historic square that's home to the **Palazzo Vecchio**. Grab a panino at **I' Girone De' Ghiotti** (Via dei Cimatori, 23r) nearby. After lunch, head to the **Uffizi Gallery** (Piazzale degli Uffizi, 6), one of the most famous art museums in the world, housing works by Botticelli, Leonardo da Vinci, and Michelangelo. You could spend hours here, but be sure not to miss **The Birth of Venus** by Botticelli.

Evening:
For your first dinner in Florence, experience a traditional **Florentine steak (Bistecca alla Fiorentina)** at **Trattoria Sostanza** (Via del Porcellana, 25r).

It's a place loved by locals and tourists alike, and its historic atmosphere is part of the charm.

Day 2: A Day of Art and History
Morning:
Dedicate your morning to one of the most famous sculptures in the world: **Michelangelo's David**. The **Galleria dell'Accademia** (Via Ricasoli, 58/60) houses this masterpiece. But, don't rush—take time to appreciate the other sculptures in the gallery, such as Michelangelo's unfinished works known as "Prisoners."

Afternoon:
Afterward, head to **Piazza Santa Croce** to visit the **Basilica di Santa Croce** (Piazza Santa Croce, 16). The church is the final resting place of many notable Italians, including Galileo and Michelangelo. The surrounding area offers a variety of cafes, perfect for a lunch break.

Evening:
For dinner, head over to the **Oltrarno District**, a quieter side of Florence. Enjoy a meal at **Osteria dell'Enoteca** (Piazza del Carmine, 5r) for a true taste of Tuscan cuisine. Afterward, if you're in the mood for some entertainment, check out a performance at the **Teatro della Pergola** (Via della Pergola, 12), Florence's oldest theater.

Day 3: Hidden Gems and Local Vibes
Morning:
Today, we're exploring the less touristy side of Florence. Start at **Basilica di San Miniato al Monte** (Via delle Porte Sante), perched atop a hill offering one of the best panoramic views of the city. After taking in the view, head to **Piazza Santo Spirito**, a charming square where locals gather for a coffee. The nearby **Piazza del Carmine** is home to the beautiful **Cappella Brancacci**, known for its stunning frescoes.

Afternoon:
Lunch is best served in a local trattoria in **San Frediano**. Afterward, explore the artisan shops and craft boutiques in this district. Take some time to discover the **Borgo San Frediano**, Florence's artisanal heart, where you'll find workshops making handmade leather goods, paper, and more.

Evening:
End your day with an aperitivo at **La Terrazza Rooftop Bar** (Hotel Continentale, Vicolo dell'Oro, 6r), where you can sip on a spritz while enjoying a view of the Ponte Vecchio and the Arno River. For dinner, enjoy a casual meal at **Trattoria 4 Leoni** (Vicolo dei Leoni, 9r), known for its excellent Tuscan dishes like pasta with pear and pecorino.

Day 4: Tuscan Day Trip - Chianti Region
Morning & Afternoon:
Take a day trip out of the city to explore the scenic **Chianti wine region**. Start with a visit to **Castello di Verrazzano** (Località Verrazzano, 6), a winery that offers tours of its vineyards, cellars, and tastings of their exceptional Chianti wines. Spend the afternoon winding through the rolling hills, stopping in charming towns like **Greve in Chianti** and **Radda in Chianti** for a taste of rural Tuscany.

Evening:
Return to Florence and unwind with a light dinner at **Il Guscio** (Borgo San Jacopo, 9), a cozy restaurant near the Arno River serving delicious Tuscan fare.

Day 5: Discovering Florence's Gardens and Views
Morning:
Spend your morning in the **Boboli Gardens** (Piazza Pitti, 1), an expansive and beautiful park behind the **Pitti Palace**. This green oasis is perfect for a relaxing stroll. Afterward, head to **Piazzale Michelangelo** for the iconic view of Florence. It's the best place to take that postcard-perfect photo of the city with the Arno River in the foreground.

Afternoon:
Visit the **Bardini Gardens** (Costa San Giorgio, 2) for a quieter, less crowded alternative. The gardens also offer fantastic views of the city and a chance to relax in nature.

Evening:
For dinner, enjoy a meal at **Cibrèo** (Via del Verrocchio, 8r), a renowned Florence institution with a modern twist on Tuscan classics.

Day 6: Shopping and More Art
Morning:
Visit the **Ponte Vecchio** and its many jewelry shops, or explore the nearby **Piazza della Repubblica** for more high-end boutiques. Florence is also home to many art galleries beyond the Uffizi, like the **Palazzo Strozzi** (Piazza Strozzi) or the **Museo del Bargello** (Via del Proconsolo, 4), a hidden gem with Renaissance sculptures.

Afternoon:
For a fun lunch, head to **Mercato Centrale** (Piazza del Mercato Centrale), where you can sample various Italian delicacies under one roof. The market has everything from fresh pasta to cured meats and artisanal cheeses.

Evening:
Wrap up the day with a casual dinner at **La Giostra** (Borgo Pinti, 12r), a beloved spot known for its rich history, warm ambiance, and hearty meals.

Day 7: Last Day - Relax and Reflect
Morning:
Spend your final day taking a leisurely stroll along the Arno River. Visit the **Rose Garden** (Viale Giuseppe Mazzini), a peaceful spot filled with fragrant blooms and spectacular views of Florence's skyline.
Afternoon:
Head back to **Piazza del Duomo** for some final shopping, or visit the **Museo**

Galileo (Piazza dei Giudici, 1), which houses incredible scientific instruments and historical exhibits.

Evening:
For your farewell dinner, dine at **La Loggia** (Viale Galileo, 2), a restaurant offering panoramic views of Florence. It's the perfect place to toast your week in this unforgettable city.

Themed Itineraries:
With so much to offer, themed itineraries are a great way to tailor your visit to your personal interests. Let's explore three unique ways to experience Florence based on what you love most!

For the Art Lovers:
Florence is often considered the birthplace of the Renaissance, and the city's art scene reflects this rich history. If you're an art lover, Florence is an absolute dream come true. From world-renowned museums to iconic pieces by Michelangelo and Botticelli, here's how to spend a day soaking up Florence's artistic treasures.

Morning:
Start your day at the **Uffizi Gallery** (Piazzale degli Uffizi, 6). It's one of the most famous art museums in the world, housing masterpieces by Botticelli, Leonardo da Vinci, and Raphael. The museum opens at 8:15 a.m. (closed Mondays), so arrive early to avoid the crowds. Don't miss **Botticelli's "The Birth of Venus"**—it's one of the most iconic pieces of art in the world, and seeing it in person is breathtaking.

Mid-Morning:
Next, take a short walk to the **Galleria dell'Accademia** (Via Ricasoli, 58/60), where you'll find Michelangelo's famous **David**. While you're there, explore other works by the master sculptor, such as the unfinished **Prisoners** sculptures that give a glimpse into Michelangelo's process. Be sure to take

time to appreciate the architecture of the gallery itself, which is housed in a former convent.

Lunch:
After a morning of art, you'll need to recharge. Head to **Trattoria ZaZa** (Piazza del Mercato Centrale), a popular spot with both locals and tourists. The **ribollita** (a traditional Tuscan soup) is a must-try, especially in cooler months.

Afternoon:
After lunch, visit the **Palazzo Pitti** (Piazza de' Pitti, 1), a former royal palace that houses multiple museums and collections, including Renaissance art and modern works. Be sure to explore the **Palatine Gallery**, which boasts works by Raphael, Titian, and Caravaggio.

End your day at the **Basilica di Santa Maria Novella** (Piazza Santa Maria Novella), where you can admire the beautiful **frescoes** by Masaccio, Ghirlandaio, and Filippino Lippi.

Why You Should Visit:
Florence offers an unparalleled journey through art history. The city's museums are home to some of the most important works of art in Western civilization. Whether you're looking to admire the works of Michelangelo or discovering lesser-known gems, Florence's art scene will captivate and inspire you.

For the Foodies:
Florence is not only a feast for the eyes but also for the palate. If you love to eat, the city will not disappoint. From traditional Tuscan dishes to world-class wines, here's how to spend a day indulging in Florence's culinary delights.

Morning:
Start your day with a typical Florentine breakfast: a **cappuccino** and a **cornetto** (Italian croissant). Head to **Caffè Gilli** (Via Roma, 1r), a historic

café that's been serving coffee since 1733. It's the perfect place to soak in the atmosphere of Florence while enjoying a pastry.

Mid-Morning:
Next, head to the **Mercato Centrale** (Piazza del Mercato Centrale), where you'll find a vibrant market filled with fresh produce, meats, cheeses, and baked goods. Take time to explore the stalls and sample local treats like **prosciutto**, **pecorino** cheese, and **truffle oil**. If you're feeling adventurous, try **lampredotto**, a Florentine street food made from the stomach of a cow. It's a local delicacy that you can find at food trucks around the market.

Lunch:
For lunch, enjoy a traditional **bistecca alla fiorentina** (Florentine steak) at **Osteria dell'Enoteca** (Piazza dei Rossi, 3), a cozy restaurant known for its Tuscan meats and fine wines. Be sure to pair your steak with a glass of local **Chianti**.

Afternoon:
After lunch, join a **food tour** to explore Florence's culinary delights. A great option is the **Florence Food Tour** which takes you through local markets, artisan food shops, and gelato stands. Don't miss the chance to taste authentic Italian **gelato** at **Gelateria dei Neri** (Via dei Neri, 20).

Why You Should Visit:
Florence offers an unforgettable culinary journey. Whether you're savoring a hearty plate of pasta, sampling local cheeses and meats, or indulging in gelato, the city is full of flavors that will leave you craving more.

For Families: Fun and Education in Florence
Florence is a fantastic destination for families, offering plenty of opportunities for both education and fun. Whether your kids are fascinated by art or just love exploring new places, Florence is full of engaging activities for all ages.

Morning:
Start your family-friendly day at the **Museo Galileo** (Piazza dei Giudici, 1).

This science museum is a hit with kids, featuring interactive exhibits about Galileo's discoveries and the history of science. It's a great way to engage children with learning in a fun environment.

Mid-Morning:
Next, head to the **Boboli Gardens** (Piazza de' Pitti, 1), where your family can explore vast green spaces, fountains, and sculptures. It's a perfect spot for a relaxed walk, and kids will love discovering hidden paths and stopping to admire the views over Florence.

Lunch:
For lunch, take the family to **La Ménagère** (Via de' Ginori, 8r), a stylish yet casual café and restaurant that's kid-friendly and serves delicious sandwiches, salads, and pastas.

Afternoon:
Spend the afternoon at the **Florence Zoo** (Via di Val d'Ambra), a great place for children to learn about animals. If your kids are more into history, visit **Palazzo Vecchio** (Piazza della Signoria), where you can take part in a family-friendly tour designed to engage younger visitors with stories of Florence's history.

End the day with a relaxing **boat ride along the Arno River**. It's a peaceful way to enjoy the city's sights, and kids will love being on the water. Several companies offer family-friendly tours, like **Firenze in Barca**.

Why You Should Visit:
Florence offers a combination of art, history, and outdoor spaces that will captivate children and adults alike. From hands-on museums to expansive gardens, there's no shortage of fun and educational activities for the whole family.

Day Trips from Florence:

The surrounding areas offer some of Italy's most iconic sights, scenic landscapes, and charming towns. If you've got a few extra days during your Florence visit, a day trip to Pisa, Siena, or the Chianti Region is a must. Here's a guide to make the most of each destination, filled with tips, personal anecdotes, and reasons to visit.

Pisa:

When most people think of Pisa, the first image that pops into their mind is the famous Leaning Tower. And for good reason—it's an iconic landmark that draws millions of visitors each year. But there's more to Pisa than just the tilted tower!

Why You Should Visit:

The Leaning Tower of Pisa is part of the *Piazza dei Miracoli* (Square of Miracles), a UNESCO World Heritage site, and one of the most beautiful piazzas in Italy. While many people rush to take the classic "holding up the tower" photo, there's plenty to explore around the square.

Activities:

- **Climb the Leaning Tower:** For the best experience, purchase tickets in advance (the climb is limited to 30 people at a time). The view from the top is breathtaking, offering a panoramic look at Pisa and the surrounding Tuscan landscape.
- **Explore the Cathedral and Baptistery:** The *Duomo di Pisa* is a stunning example of Romanesque architecture. Afterward, visit the *Baptistery*, famous for its acoustics. If you're lucky, you might hear a live demonstration of its unique echoing sound.
- **Stroll Through Pisa's Streets:** After taking your photos and exploring the main sights, wander through the quaint streets of Pisa. Stop by one of the many charming cafes for a coffee and enjoy the local atmosphere.

Practical Tips:
- **How to Get There:** Pisa is about an hour's drive or a 1-hour train ride from Florence. If you're traveling by train, Pisa's station is located 15 minutes walking from the Piazza dei Miracoli.
- **When to Visit:** The best time to visit is early in the morning or later in the afternoon to avoid the crowds.

Siena:
Siena, often described as one of Tuscany's most picturesque medieval towns, offers a completely different vibe compared to Florence. Its cobblestone streets, historic palaces, and *Piazza del Campo* will transport you back in time.

Why You Should Visit:
Siena is famous for its well-preserved medieval architecture and the *Palio di Siena*, a thrilling horse race that takes place every summer. But even outside of race season, Siena offers a rich history and some of the most beautiful views in Tuscany.

Activities:
- **Piazza del Campo:** The heart of Siena, this shell-shaped square hosts the famous Palio horse race. Even if you're not there for the event, the square is a great place to people-watch and grab a gelato while soaking in the atmosphere.
- **Visit the Siena Cathedral (Duomo di Siena):** The cathedral is a masterpiece of Italian Gothic architecture, known for its black-and-white striped facade and stunning interior, including the *Piccolomini Library*.
- **Explore the Narrow Streets:** Siena's medieval streets are perfect for leisurely strolls. Take time to explore the *Contrada* (neighborhoods) and discover hidden churches, artisan shops, and local eateries.
- **Wine Tasting:** Siena is in the heart of Tuscany's wine region, so don't miss the chance to visit a local vineyard for a wine-tasting session.

Practical Tips:
- **How to Get There:** Siena is about 1.5 hours by bus or car from Florence. The bus station is located just outside the historical center, but it's still a short walk to the main attractions.
- **When to Visit:** Siena is a year-round destination, but to experience the Palio, visit in July or August. The town gets especially busy during these months, so be prepared for crowds.

The Chianti Region:
If you've dreamed of winding roads through rolling hills, vineyards, and cypress trees, then a trip to the Chianti region is what you're looking for. Located between Florence and Siena, Chianti is renowned for its wine production, charming villages, and breathtaking landscapes.

Why You Should Visit:
Chianti is Tuscany's wine-producing heart, and visiting the region gives you a chance to taste some of the best wines in the world, set against the backdrop of the picturesque countryside. It's the perfect destination if you're looking for a slower-paced day trip that allows you to enjoy nature, culture, and delicious food.

Activities:
- **Wine Tours and Tastings:** Chianti is famous for its *Chianti Classico* wine, and many wineries offer tours where you can learn about the wine-making process and taste local wines. Be sure to try the *Riserva* for a special treat. One of the best-known vineyards in the area is *Castello di Verrazzano*, offering both wine tours and cooking classes.
- **Explore Greve in Chianti:** This charming town is the gateway to the Chianti region and is known for its picturesque square and wine shops. It's the perfect spot for a leisurely lunch or to pick up a bottle of local wine to take home.
- **Hiking and Cycling:** For outdoor lovers, Chianti offers plenty of hiking and cycling paths that let you explore its vineyards and olive groves in peace.

- **Visit Castles and Villas:** Many castles and villas dot the Chianti landscape. Some offer tours and host events, such as *Castello di Brolio*, a stunning estate with a rich history and panoramic views.

Practical Tips:
- **How to Get There:** The Chianti region is about an hour's drive from Florence. If you don't have a car, consider joining a guided wine tour that includes transportation, or take a bus to Greve in Chianti.
- **When to Visit:** The region is beautiful year-round, but spring and fall are especially magical. The harvest season, around late September to October, is a great time to visit vineyards and participate in local wine festivals.

How to Personalize Your Own Itinerary

While many travelers stick to the must-see attractions, like the Duomo or the Uffizi Gallery, customizing your itinerary can allow you to experience Florence in a deeper, more meaningful way. Whether you're an art lover, a foodie, or someone who simply enjoys wandering off the beaten path, here's how to craft an itinerary that's tailored just for you.

1. Reflect on Your Interests

The first step to personalizing your itinerary is to reflect on what excites you most about Florence. Are you in Florence for the art? The food? The history? The shopping? The natural beauty?

For example, if you're drawn to art, you'll want to prioritize Florence's incredible museums and galleries, like the **Uffizi Gallery** (Piazzale degli Uffizi, 6, Florence), home to Botticelli's *The Birth of Venus* and da Vinci's *Annunciation*. You might also want to explore the lesser-known **Bargello Museum** (Via del Proconsolo, 4, Florence), with its Renaissance sculptures by Donatello.

If food is more your thing, Florence offers countless opportunities to indulge. Head over to **Mercato Centrale** (Piazza del Mercato Centrale, Florence) for an authentic food market experience, where you can sample local cheeses, wines, and truffle-infused delicacies. For something a bit more refined, book a **cooking class** at **Cucina Lorenzo de' Medici** to learn how to prepare classic Florentine dishes like *bistecca alla fiorentina*.

2. Set a Realistic Timeline

Next, think about how much time you have in the city and how much you can realistically do. Florence is a small, walkable city, but there's still a lot to see. If you have just one day, stick to the highlights—don't try to squeeze in too much.

For example, an itinerary for one day could look like this:

- **Morning:** Visit the **Duomo**, including the Baptistry and the dome climb (allow around 2-3 hours).
- **Afternoon:** Explore **Piazza della Signoria**, the **Palazzo Vecchio**, and **Uffizi Gallery** (another 3 hours or so).
- **Evening:** Enjoy a leisurely dinner at a classic **Bouchon** like **Trattoria ZaZa** (Piazza del Mercato Centrale, 26r, Florence) and stroll around **Ponte Vecchio** after dark.

For those with more time, consider adding half-day trips to nearby towns, like **Siena** or **Pisa**, or venturing into the **Chianti wine region** for a vineyard tour.

3. Mix Popular Sites with Hidden Gems

A major part of personalizing your itinerary is balancing the well-known attractions with some off-the-beaten-path gems. Sure, the **Ponte Vecchio** (Ponte Vecchio, Florence), with its iconic gold shops, is a must-see, but nearby **Borgo San Jacopo** offers charming streets with local shops and fewer crowds.

Another hidden gem? **Santo Spirito**, a lively neighborhood located just across the river in **Oltrarno**. The **Piazza Santo Spirito** (Florence) is a perfect place to enjoy a coffee and people-watch, while **Basilica Santo Spirito** (Piazza Santo Spirito, Florence) is a stunning church that isn't as crowded as the Duomo.

Consider taking a short walk through **Giardino Bardini** (Costa San Giorgio, 2, Florence), an exquisite, less touristy garden with sweeping views over Florence and the Arno River. It's an ideal spot for a quiet afternoon after a busy morning at the museums.

4. Incorporate Local Experiences and Activities

One of the best ways to truly experience Florence is by integrating local activities into your itinerary. Florence's culinary scene is a huge part of its charm, and a cooking class or a food tour is a fantastic way to get hands-on with the local culture.

Join a **Florence Food Tour**, where you'll wander through the city's markets and eateries while tasting Florence's best bites. Or, book a **wine tasting** experience to discover the renowned Chianti wines produced just outside of the city.

For a more intimate experience, consider a **private walking tour** with a local guide, where you can focus on a specific theme that interests you, like Renaissance history, the Medici family, or Florence's street art scene.

5. Plan Around Festivals and Events

Florence's calendar is packed with events and festivals, many of which provide a unique lens through which to experience the city. The **Calcio Storico** (Historic Football) tournament, held in **Piazza Santa Croce** every June, is an incredible spectacle of tradition and competition. If you're in town during this event, make sure to plan your itinerary around the festivities.

Likewise, if you're in Florence in the winter, try to catch the **Festa di San Giovanni** (Feast of St. John), Florence's patron saint, which includes fireworks, parades, and concerts in late June.

6. Prioritize Downtime and Flexibility

When personalizing your itinerary, remember to include downtime. Florence, with its cobblestone streets, vibrant cafes, and hidden gardens, is a city made for leisurely exploration. Spend an hour just relaxing at **Caffè Gilli** (Via Roma, 1r, Florence) or **La Ménagère** (Via de' Ginori, 8r, Florence), two of the best places to sit and enjoy the Florence atmosphere.

If you've planned a day that feels too packed, it's okay to adjust. Florence is a city that invites wandering, and you'll often stumble upon unexpected surprises—whether it's an artisan workshop, a local trattoria, or a hidden viewpoint with an incredible view.

7. Mix and Match Itineraries

Lastly, the beauty of Florence lies in its variety. Want to see the classics but also delve into local life? Mix a visit to the **Accademia Gallery** with a trip to **Cappella Brancacci** for its extraordinary frescoes. Spend an afternoon exploring the **Pitti Palace** and then take a sunset stroll through **Piazzale Michelangelo** for an unforgettable view of the city.

Don't be afraid to experiment and combine experiences that interest you. Florence is a place where art, food, history, and people converge, and your itinerary should reflect that intersection.

Practical Information and Travel Tips

Getting Around:

Florence, though compact and walkable, offers several ways to get around. Whether you're strolling through the cobbled streets, hopping on a bus, or taking a leisurely bike ride, there's a simple method of transport for every type of traveler. Getting around in Florence is a breeze once you get the hang of it. Let's dive into how you can navigate this stunning city, while making the most of its rich history and vibrant atmosphere.

Walking:
The best way to experience Florence is on foot. With most of the major sights like the Duomo, Uffizi Gallery, and Ponte Vecchio all within walking distance of each other, you'll find that exploring on foot is not only the most convenient but also the most rewarding way to discover the city. Florence's historic center is small enough to wander from one iconic landmark to the next in just a few hours.

As you walk, take your time. The beauty of Florence lies in its details—small shops tucked in narrow alleys, an old street lamp hanging over a bustling square, or a hidden café with the perfect view of the Arno River. You'll stumble upon unexpected gems, like artisan shops offering handmade leather goods or quiet gardens where you can relax after a day of sightseeing.

One of my favorite things to do when visiting Florence is to walk along the riverbanks of the Arno, especially around sunset. The city's famous bridges, such as Ponte Vecchio and Ponte Santa Trinita, offer fantastic views of the city's skyline and the soft light of the setting sun reflecting off the water. It's a peaceful escape from the busy crowds of tourists. If you're up for it, take a slow walk up to Piazzale Michelangelo for a panoramic view of Florence—you'll be rewarded with one of the best vistas of the city.

Public Transport:
Although Florence is a small city, there are times when a little help from public transport can be useful—especially if you need to travel beyond the historic center, like visiting the Fiesole hills or the outer districts of the city. Florence's public transportation system is efficient and straightforward, with buses and trams connecting the central areas to more distant neighborhoods.

Buses are the most common form of public transport in Florence. The main bus network is managed by *ATAF*, and tickets can be bought at kiosks, vending machines, or directly from the bus driver. Tickets are typically valid for 90 minutes after purchase, and prices are quite reasonable, usually around 1.50€ per ride. If you plan to use public transport multiple times during your stay, a day pass might be a better deal—usually around 5€.

For most tourists, taking the bus might not be necessary if you're staying in the center, but if you want to venture out to places like the Florence American Cemetery or the Boboli Gardens, the bus can save you time. I once hopped on a bus to visit the charming district of San Frediano. It was a short ride, but it took me to a completely different side of Florence—one that isn't on most tourist itineraries, with its lively cafés and old-school charm.

Trams are a newer addition to Florence's public transport system, and they offer a smooth and reliable way to travel around the city. The tram network is especially handy for reaching places like the *Careggi* hospital or *Novoli* district, which are a bit far from the city center. The trams are clean, modern, and well-signposted. A single tram ride costs about the same as a bus ride, but there are fewer tram routes, so they might not be as convenient if you're sticking to the city's historic core.

Cycling:

If you want to explore Florence at your own pace, **cycling** is a great option. The city has several bike rental shops, and some even offer electric bikes, which can be a lifesaver for tackling the city's occasional hills. In fact, I rented a bike during my first trip to Florence and spent the day riding around the Cascine Park—Florence's largest green space. It was a refreshing way to escape the crowds and enjoy a different side of the city. Florence has been gradually improving its cycling infrastructure, with more bike lanes and bike-sharing options. *Mobike* and *Lime* are two popular bike-sharing services, allowing you to rent bikes and e-scooters for a few euros per ride. You'll find them scattered around the historic center, and they're perfect for short trips to places like Piazzale Michelangelo or the Boboli Gardens. Just remember to wear a helmet if you're riding around—safety first!

Taxis and Ride-Hailing Services

While taxis aren't as commonly used by tourists in Florence as in larger cities, they can still be helpful if you have heavy luggage or if you're staying in a more remote area. You can hail a taxi on the street or find one at the central taxi ranks, usually near train stations or major squares like Piazza del Duomo.

Alternatively, **ride-hailing services** like Uber or Lyft are also available, although they're not as widespread as in other major cities. You'll find it a bit easier to use these services when you're heading to or from the airport or if you're in a rush.

Florence's ZTL Zones

One thing to keep in mind when getting around Florence is the **ZTL** (Zona a Traffico Limitato)—a restricted traffic zone that covers the city center. Only residents, authorized vehicles, and delivery trucks can drive through these zones. If you're driving, make sure to avoid entering these areas to avoid hefty fines. The good news is that, for most visitors, walking, cycling, or using public transport is more than enough to get around.

Safety Tips for Travelers

Florence is one of the most enchanting cities in the world, with its cobbled streets, stunning architecture, and rich history. But like any popular destination, it's important to stay mindful of your surroundings to ensure your trip goes smoothly. Fortunately, Florence is generally a safe city, and with a little awareness, you can focus on enjoying your travels without worry. Here are some practical safety tips that will help keep you safe while exploring this beautiful city.

1. Pickpockets in Tourist Areas

Florence is a city that attracts millions of tourists every year, which unfortunately makes it a target for pickpockets. The most common places where these thieves operate are crowded areas like the Duomo, Ponte Vecchio, and around the Uffizi Gallery. The good news is that these crimes are usually non-violent, but losing your wallet, phone, or passport can quickly turn a dream trip into a stressful situation.

Tip: Always be aware of your surroundings, especially in busy areas. Keep your valuables in front pockets or a cross-body bag that zips shut. Avoid carrying all your important documents and cash in one place. If you need to carry a wallet, consider a money belt or an anti-theft backpack. One of the best personal anecdotes I can share is from my last trip to Florence: I made it a habit to check my bag every few minutes while walking through busy markets. It became second nature, and it really helped me stay alert.

2. Walking at Night

Florence is a beautiful city to explore at night, with its charming streets lit by soft, golden lights. However, like any city, certain areas can feel quieter and less safe after dark, particularly around the outskirts or near poorly lit alleys.

Tip: Stick to well-populated and brightly lit streets after dark. Avoid isolated areas, especially when traveling alone. If you're walking back to your accommodation late at night, try to take a taxi or rideshare. On one occasion, a friend of mine took a slightly longer walk back to their hotel after dinner and ended up in a poorly lit area; they quickly realized they should have taken a taxi. It was a wake-up call for all of us!

3. Avoiding Scams

While Florence is generally safe, there are a few scams to watch out for, particularly targeting unsuspecting tourists. Some common scams include street vendors who aggressively try to sell you items or "fortune-tellers" who will approach you, give you a "free" gift, and then demand money for it.
Tip: Be cautious when approached by strangers selling things or offering services. It's best to politely decline and walk away. If you're offered a "gift" or a free reading, don't fall for it. I once had an experience where a "fortune-teller" handed me a bracelet and then asked for a hefty sum in return. A quick, firm "no" and walking away was all it took to handle the situation.

4. Use Common Sense in Restaurants and Cafes

While Florence is known for its delicious cuisine and vibrant café culture, it's important to stay cautious when dining out. Some restaurants near tourist attractions may overcharge or even try to sneak in extra charges.

Tip: Always check the menu before ordering and ask for the price of specials or items that aren't listed. If you're unsure, it's perfectly fine to ask for a breakdown of the bill. I learned this lesson the hard way on my first trip when a small café charged me for bread that I hadn't ordered! Since then, I always ask about any extra fees before I dive into the food.

5. Be Careful with Public Transportation

Florence has a reliable public transport system, but it's always a good idea to stay vigilant, especially during rush hours or when boarding crowded buses and trams. A few travel friends of mine had their phones swiped while boarding a packed tram. The pickpockets usually work in groups, creating a distraction to grab your belongings.

Tip: When on public transport, keep your belongings close and don't let your phone or wallet hang loosely from your bag. I like to make it a habit of holding my bag tightly or, better yet, placing it in my front pocket when I'm on a busy tram or bus.

6. Stay Hydrated and Protect Yourself from the Sun
Florence can get quite hot, especially during the summer months. With so much to see and do, it's easy to forget to stay hydrated or protect yourself from the sun, which can lead to sunburn or dehydration.
Tip: Always carry a bottle of water, and make sure to apply sunscreen regularly, even if it's cloudy. The sun in Tuscany can be deceptively strong. I once skipped sunscreen while walking around Florence in the summer and ended up with a sunburn that made it hard to enjoy the rest of my trip. Don't make the same mistake!

7. Emergency Contacts and Health Care
While the chances of needing medical assistance are slim, it's always a good idea to be prepared. Florence has excellent healthcare facilities, and pharmacies are widespread. However, knowing the emergency numbers and having a few basics can go a long way if something unexpected happens.

Tip: The emergency number in Italy is 112. It's a universal number for all emergencies, from medical to fire to police. Pharmacies are marked with a green cross and are easy to find. I always make sure to know where the nearest pharmacy or hospital is, just in case. It's a small step that can offer peace of mind during your travels.

Budgeting for Florence:
Florence is one of those cities that can feel a bit pricey—especially if you're eager to experience its world-class art, history, and cuisine. But don't let that scare you! With some careful planning and insider tips, you can enjoy this beautiful city without blowing your budget. Here's how to make the most of your money while soaking in all the treasures Florence has to offer.

1. Plan Your Attractions Wisely
One of the biggest expenses in Florence is admission to its iconic museums and landmarks. The Uffizi Gallery, the Accademia, and the Duomo all charge hefty entry fees. However, there are a few ways to save:

- **Free Days**: Many museums in Florence offer free entry on certain days or evenings. For example, the Uffizi Gallery offers free entry on the first Sunday of every month. It's a great way to see the masterpieces without the ticket price. Just be prepared for crowds—Florence is a popular destination year-round, and free days can get busy.
- **Combined Tickets**: If you're planning to visit several museums, consider purchasing a combined ticket. For instance, a single ticket for the Uffizi, Palazzo Pitti, and Boboli Gardens allows you to visit all three for a reduced rate, saving you money compared to buying separate tickets.
- **Florence Card**: The Florence Card is a pass that gives you access to over 70 museums and sites in Florence. While it may seem pricey at first glance, it can be worth it if you plan to visit many of the city's top attractions. The card also allows you to skip some of the long lines, which is a huge time-saver.

2. Eat Like a Local
Dining in Florence can be expensive, especially if you're eating at tourist hotspots. However, there are plenty of ways to enjoy delicious, authentic meals without breaking the bank:

- **Eat at Local Trattorias and Osterias**: Avoid the high-priced restaurants in the main squares, and instead head to local trattorias and osterias where you'll get home-cooked meals for a fraction of the price. Places like *Trattoria da Burde* or *Osteria Santo Spirito* offer amazing traditional Florentine dishes like *ribollita* (a Tuscan vegetable soup) and *bistecca alla Fiorentina* at reasonable prices.
- **Street Food**: Florence has an amazing street food scene. Don't miss out on the famous *lampredotto* (a sandwich made from cow's stomach), which is served from food trucks around the city. For

just a few euros, you'll get a tasty, filling meal that reflects the city's culinary history. Try it at *L'Antico Trippaio* in the San Frediano district.
- **Markets for Fresh Ingredients**: Florence's food markets are not only perfect for experiencing local culture, but they're also budget-friendly. The *Mercato Centrale* offers fresh produce, meats, cheeses, and other local specialties that you can take back to your apartment if you're staying somewhere with a kitchen. This is a great option if you want to cook some meals yourself.

3. Skip the Tourist Traps

As tempting as they may be, touristy restaurants, souvenir shops, and overpriced cafés can drain your wallet. Instead, follow these tips to get the best experiences without overpaying:
- **Cafés**: Avoid sitting down in cafés located near major tourist attractions like the Duomo. These often have inflated prices for basic coffee or pastries. Instead, grab a coffee standing at the bar like the locals do. This is a much cheaper option and an excellent way to experience Florence like a true Florentine.
- **Souvenirs**: The city is filled with souvenir shops, but many of them charge inflated prices for mass-produced items. If you're looking for authentic and unique souvenirs, venture into artisan shops in areas like the Oltrarno district. You can find beautiful leather goods, hand-painted ceramics, and original artworks at fair prices.

4. Walk or Use Public Transport

Florence is a walkable city, so take advantage of the fact that most of the major attractions are within walking distance of each other. Walking is not only free but also allows you to experience the city in a more intimate and personal way.

However, if you need to get around and walking isn't an option, public transport is affordable and efficient. The city has buses and trams that cover the most popular areas. A single bus ticket costs just €1.50, and a day pass is available for €5, which is a great deal if you plan on using public transport multiple times in one day.

5. Stay Smart with Accommodation
Although you asked for no section on accommodation, it's worth noting that where you stay can have a huge impact on your budget. While Florence has some luxurious hotels, there are plenty of affordable options too:
- **Stay Outside the Historic Center**: Hotels in the historic center are often expensive, but if you're willing to stay a bit further out, you can find more affordable options. Areas like the *San Frediano* or *Campo di Marte* districts offer great places to stay for a lower cost, with easy access to the city center via public transport.
- **Airbnb and Hostels**: For even more affordable options, look into renting an apartment via Airbnb or staying in one of Florence's budget-friendly hostels. These choices can offer a more homey experience while saving you money.

6. Look for Discounts and Deals
Florence is packed with experiences that don't cost much (or anything at all). Some ways to enjoy the city on a budget include:
- **Free Walking Tours**: Florence offers several free walking tours, where you can tip the guide at the end. These tours are a great way to learn about the city's history and major landmarks without paying for an official guide.
- **Public Gardens**: Florence has several lovely public gardens, including the *Giardino delle Rose* and *Giardino Bardini*, where you can relax and enjoy stunning views of the city for free or for just a small fee.

Health and Wellness:
When traveling in Florence, taking care of your health and well-being is important. Whether it's a minor scrape from exploring the cobblestone streets or needing medication for something more serious, understanding how to access healthcare and wellness services will ensure you have a

smooth experience. Thankfully, Florence is well-equipped with pharmacies, emergency services, and resources for travelers who need medical assistance.

Pharmacies in Florence:
Florence's pharmacies are easy to spot with their distinctive green crosses illuminated at night. Pharmacies here are not just places to pick up prescriptions, but they often carry over-the-counter medication, skincare products, and even some wellness items like herbal remedies.
Most pharmacies in Florence are open during standard business hours—typically from 9:00 AM to 1:00 PM and then again from 4:00 PM to 7:30 PM. On Sundays and holidays, many pharmacies are closed, but there is always a rotating *farmacia di turno* (on-call pharmacy) open for emergencies. You'll see signs outside pharmacies indicating the nearest one that is on duty, so if you need something urgently, just look for the green cross or check with your hotel concierge.

One thing to note is that, in Italy, pharmacies operate with a slightly different system than in some other countries. If you need a specific prescription medication, you'll likely need to visit a doctor first. However, many basic over-the-counter items like pain relievers, cold medicine, and bandages are available without a prescription.

I remember a time when I was in Florence during the winter, and I came down with a nasty cold. My hotel receptionist helped me find the nearest pharmacy, where I picked up everything I needed for a speedy recovery. The pharmacist was incredibly friendly and spoke English, which made it even easier for me to explain what I was experiencing. It's this kind of customer service that makes Florence feel like home.

What to Bring for Your Health and Wellness
Before you travel, it's always a good idea to bring your regular medications and any specific health-related items you use, such as allergy medicine or vitamins. Florence has modern pharmacies, but not every pharmacy may

carry the exact brands or formulations you're used to, especially for specialty items.

A small first aid kit can go a long way. Basic items like band-aids, antiseptic cream, and pain relievers will help with minor accidents. In case of an emergency, knowing where the nearest pharmacy is, especially near your accommodation, will save you time.

Also, don't forget to pack any necessary travel health insurance documentation, especially if you have ongoing medical needs or pre-existing conditions. It's good to have coverage that can help with doctor visits or prescriptions while traveling.

Emergency Contacts in Florence
While Florence is generally a safe city, knowing how to handle an emergency is always important. Below are some key emergency contacts that can be very helpful during your visit:
- **Emergency Number in Italy:** The emergency number for medical, fire, or police emergencies is **112**. This is the same throughout Europe, so if you're traveling within the EU, this is a number you can easily remember.
- **Ambulance:** For immediate medical help, you can call **118**. An ambulance will be dispatched quickly for serious accidents or health emergencies. English is commonly spoken by emergency responders, but if you feel more comfortable with Italian, knowing a few key phrases like "Ho bisogno di un'ambulanza" (I need an ambulance) can be helpful.
- **Police:** The police can be reached by dialing **113**. While Florence is a generally safe city, it's still important to be aware of your surroundings, especially in busy tourist areas.

I once had to use the emergency number when I witnessed a small accident while exploring the historic center. The process was quick and efficient, and the emergency services were on-site within minutes. Thankfully, the situation wasn't too serious, but it was reassuring to know the system worked smoothly.

Health Clinics and Doctors

For non-emergency health issues, Florence offers several medical centers and private clinics. If you're feeling unwell and need to see a doctor but don't need immediate emergency assistance, you can visit one of these clinics. Many clinics will accept walk-ins, but it's a good idea to call ahead if possible to avoid long waits.

Most general practitioners in Florence are able to speak English, especially in the more tourist-centric areas, but it's always wise to check beforehand. You may be required to pay upfront for a consultation, and your travel insurance might reimburse you later. If you're in need of medical advice or a prescription, many pharmacies also offer services where they can refer you to a local doctor if needed.

Wellness Options in Florence

Florence is not just about art and history—it's also a city that celebrates wellness. From luxurious spas to yoga studios, the city has options for those who want to unwind, de-stress, or pamper themselves. Many spas offer relaxing massages, facials, and treatments that use local ingredients like olive oil and thermal water.

If you're into fitness, you'll find several gyms and yoga studios around the city. Florence also has a mild climate, which is perfect for outdoor activities. You could join a walking or cycling tour to explore the city or simply take a stroll in the Boboli Gardens or along the Arno River. These outdoor activities not only keep you active but also provide a great way to relax and take in the beautiful sights of Florence.

Accessibility Information

Florence is a city of winding streets, cobbled alleys, and charming piazzas, which makes it a bit tricky to navigate for visitors with mobility challenges. However, it's also a city that has been increasingly making efforts to improve accessibility, ensuring that all visitors can experience its art, culture, and beauty. Whether you're traveling with a wheelchair, using a cane, or need additional assistance, there are plenty of options to help make your trip more enjoyable.

Getting Around Florence:
Florence's historic center is relatively compact, which means many of its major attractions are within walking distance. However, navigating the narrow, uneven cobblestone streets can be a challenge for those with mobility difficulties.

Public Transport: Florence's public transport system is operated by **ATAF**, which includes buses and trams. The good news is that many of the trams and buses are accessible to wheelchair users. Trams, in particular, are equipped with low floors for easy access, and there are spaces reserved for wheelchairs. The buses, while not all the same, have designated spots for wheelchairs as well. The **Santa Maria Novella Train Station** is also fully accessible, with elevators, ramps, and accessible toilets.

Taxis: Florence also offers accessible taxis for travelers with mobility challenges. These taxis are specially designed to accommodate wheelchairs. You can request an accessible taxi by calling **055 4242**, or you can simply find them at designated taxi stands in key areas of the city. While taxis are a convenient option for getting around, they may be pricier than public transport, so it's always good to plan ahead.

Getting to Attractions:
While many of Florence's main attractions are easily accessible, a few do have challenges due to their age and location. But don't let that deter you—there are solutions to make these iconic spots easier to navigate.

- **The Duomo (Cathedral of Santa Maria del Fiore):** The Duomo itself is wheelchair accessible, with an entrance at **Piazza del Duomo** that provides a ramp for those with limited mobility. However, keep in mind that the climb to the dome, which is one of Florence's most famous experiences, is not wheelchair accessible, as it involves narrow, steep stairs. But you can still enjoy the beauty of the cathedral from the ground level, which is a spectacle in itself.
- **Uffizi Gallery:** This world-renowned art museum has been renovated to improve accessibility. The museum has elevators, and there are ramps to help visitors with mobility challenges get

around. The galleries are spacious, making it easier to navigate with a wheelchair or a walker. It's worth noting that some of the rooms might be a bit tighter during peak tourist seasons, so planning your visit for early morning or late afternoon can help avoid crowds.
- **Ponte Vecchio:** One of Florence's most famous landmarks, the **Ponte Vecchio**, is a beautiful bridge lined with jewelry shops. While it's historic and somewhat narrow, the bridge is mostly accessible, with ramps at both ends of the bridge. However, due to its popularity, it can get crowded, so if you're visiting during peak hours, be prepared for slow movement.
- **Boboli Gardens:** While Boboli Gardens are one of Florence's most stunning outdoor spaces, they present a challenge for wheelchair users due to the sloping hills and uneven terrain. However, there are parts of the garden that are more accessible, especially near the entrance and the first few terraces. If you still wish to experience the entire garden, consider renting an electric wheelchair or scooter from local providers, which can make your visit much easier.

Accessibility at Restaurants and Hotels:
Florence's restaurant scene is full of charm, but the older buildings sometimes make it difficult to find fully accessible entrances. Many of the more modern eateries in Florence have made sure that their doors are wide enough and offer ramps for wheelchair users. Some restaurants in the **Oltrarno** district, for example, are located in older buildings, so you may have to plan for steps, but don't hesitate to ask the staff for assistance—they're often willing to help.
When it comes to accommodation, many hotels are increasingly becoming more accessible, with ramps, wider doors, and elevators for easier access to higher floors. Larger hotels, especially those located near **Piazza della Signoria** or the **Santa Maria Novella Train Station**, are more likely to have these accommodations. It's always wise to call ahead to ensure the hotel's specific amenities suit your needs.

Public Restrooms:
Many of the public restrooms in Florence's central areas are accessible, and the majority of attractions also have accessible facilities. The **FirenzeCard** (a pass that grants access to most museums and sites) can also help you identify the most accessible venues, as it provides detailed information about services like elevators and wheelchair ramps.

Practical Tips:
- **Accessible Tours:** Several local tour operators offer guided tours with accessible transportation. These tours can be a great way to see the city while avoiding the hassle of navigating narrow streets or climbing stairs. For example, **Tuscany by Taxi** offers accessible private tours with a vehicle equipped for wheelchairs.
- **Renting Mobility Equipment:** If you need a wheelchair, scooter, or other mobility aids, Florence has several shops that can rent out equipment. Companies like **Florence Mobility** can deliver and pick up equipment directly at your hotel.
- **Weather Considerations:** Florence can get quite hot in the summer, which may be challenging for those with mobility issues. Be sure to stay hydrated, wear comfortable shoes, and take breaks in shaded spots, especially when navigating outdoor spaces like gardens or the city's cobbled streets.

Important Numbers and Local Contacts

While Florence is a beautiful city to explore, like any destination, it's always good to be prepared and know who to call if you run into any unexpected situations. Whether you're in need of emergency assistance, looking for a reliable taxi, or just need help navigating the local system, this list of important numbers and contacts will help ensure your time in Florence is smooth and enjoyable.

Emergency Services

1. **Police**:

- **Number**: 113
- In case of a crime, emergency, or if you're in need of general law enforcement assistance, the national police can be reached by dialing 113. Florence, like much of Italy, is generally very safe, but it's always wise to be prepared. I remember one time I accidentally dropped my wallet in a crowded Piazza del Duomo and had it returned to me by a kind passerby. The local police station is very supportive and responsive, even for minor incidents.

2. **Ambulance/Medical Emergency**:

   - **Number**: 118
   - For any medical emergencies, whether it's a sudden illness or an accident, dialing 118 will connect you directly to an ambulance service. Florence's hospitals are well-equipped and offer excellent care, but if you're unfamiliar with the area, don't hesitate to reach out for immediate help. I once saw a tourist collapse due to heat exhaustion on a summer day in Piazza Santa Croce, and within minutes, paramedics arrived and took care of everything.

3. **Fire Department**:

   - **Number**: 115
   - Fires are rare, but it's always reassuring to know that the firefighters in Florence are just a call away. They respond quickly and are well-trained, especially in a city with so many historic buildings and delicate structures. If you're staying in an older building or a traditional residence, it's a good idea to know the location of the nearest exit and how to act in case of a fire.

Medical Assistance and Pharmacies

1. **General Medical Assistance:**
   - **Number:** 055 794 8310 (Florence Health Center)
   - If you're feeling unwell or need general medical advice during your trip, the Florence Health Center is a good place to start. They provide both emergency and routine care, and many doctors speak English. I once had a minor ear infection during a trip to Florence, and the staff at the health center were very helpful in giving me a quick diagnosis and the treatment I needed. Keep in mind that pharmacies (Farmacie) are quite common in Florence, and many are open 24/7, offering over-the-counter remedies.

2. **Pharmacies (Farmacie):**
   - Pharmacies are an integral part of Florence's cityscape, and you'll find one on nearly every corner. If you need medication or just some advice about minor health issues, you can stop by any of the local pharmacies. The red cross symbol on the green or white sign is an easy indicator. For non-urgent issues, Florence also has plenty of "Parafarmacie," which offer personal care products but without the need for a prescription.
   - **Emergency Pharmacy (Farmacia di Turno):**
     - **Number:** 055 210 100 (Emergency service)
     - If you're looking for a pharmacy that's open during odd hours, you'll find one on rotation, available even on holidays. Keep an eye out for the "Farmacia di Turno" signs posted outside pharmacies to know where to go.

Transport and Taxis

1. **Taxis**:

   - **Number**: 055 4242 or 055 4390

   - While Florence is a walkable city, you may occasionally need a taxi for trips outside the city center or to the airport. These numbers are for the two main taxi companies in Florence. I've used taxis a few times to get back to my hotel after a late dinner in the Oltrarno district, and the drivers are always friendly, knowledgeable, and ready to give helpful tips about the city. Keep in mind that taxis are more expensive than public transport, so use them sparingly if you're on a budget.

2. **Public Transport (ATAF)**:

   - **Number**: 800 424 500 (Information Line)

   - Florence has an efficient bus system, but it can be a bit confusing at first. The ATAF public transport service covers the entire city, and if you're not sure which bus to take, this is your go-to number for assistance. The staff at ATAF is helpful and will gladly guide you in English. Whether you're heading to a museum or out to one of the scenic hills around Florence, you can rely on public buses for an affordable way to get around.

Tourist Assistance and Information

1. **Florence Tourist Information (IAT)**:

   - **Number**: 055 290 832

   - If you have any questions about Florence, this is the number for the official tourist information center. They can provide you with maps, event schedules, and advice on local attractions. I remember stopping by their main office near the Duomo, where they gave me a free map and insider tips on places to eat in the Oltrarno district, which turned out to be some of my best meals during my trip!

2. **Florence City Hall**:

    - **Number**: 055 276 61

    - For any general inquiries about city services, permits, or even local regulations, you can contact the Florence City Hall. Their team can also help with non-tourist-related matters, like parking or civic events. Florence's government is generally very accommodating and friendly, and I found their office to be quite efficient when I needed to sort out a small issue with my parking ticket.

Emergency Support for Tourists

1. **Tourist Police (Polizia Municipale)**:

    - **Number**: 055 234 0180

    - If you ever feel unsafe or need immediate assistance while traveling in Florence, the tourist police are there to help. They have a dedicated team for tourists, which means they speak multiple languages, including English, and are familiar with common issues faced by visitors, such as lost items or disturbances.

Appendices and Useful Resources

List of Must-Have Apps for Florence Travel

When you're exploring a city as rich in history and culture as Florence, a little tech can go a long way. From navigating the city's winding streets to discovering hidden gems, there are several apps that can make your trip smoother and more enjoyable. Whether you're a first-time visitor or a seasoned traveler, here's a list of must-have apps to help you get the most out of your time in Florence.

1. Google Maps:

It's hard to beat Google Maps when it comes to navigating a new city. Florence's narrow streets, especially in the historic center, can be tricky to navigate, but Google Maps will help you get from the Duomo to the Ponte Vecchio without missing a beat.

I remember getting lost on my first visit, trying to find a quaint café tucked away in the Oltrarno district. After a few wrong turns, I opened up Google Maps and was able to find my way quickly. It even offers walking directions, public transport options, and nearby attractions, so you don't have to worry about being late for your next gallery tour.

Pro Tip: Download the map offline before your trip so that you don't run into connectivity issues while wandering the city. Florence has great Wi-Fi, but having offline access will save you time and hassle.

2. TheFork (formerly EasyTable):

Florence is home to some of the best dining experiences in Italy, from casual trattorias to fine dining spots. TheFork allows you to browse restaurant menus, make reservations, and read reviews from fellow travelers and locals. This app is invaluable for avoiding the disappointment of turning up at a fully-booked restaurant, especially in Florence's more popular areas.

On my last trip, I used TheFork to book a last-minute table at a hidden gem called Trattoria Sostanza, famous for its butter chicken. The service was impeccable, and without the app, I probably wouldn't have known about it or secured a seat.

Pro Tip: Keep an eye out for exclusive deals and discounts, as some restaurants offer promotions for app users, which can make your meal even more enjoyable (and affordable!).

3. Rick Steves Audio Europe:

If you're not keen on hiring a guide but still want to experience Florence through expert eyes, Rick Steves Audio Europe is a fantastic option. The app offers free audio tours for some of Florence's major attractions, including the Uffizi Gallery and the Duomo. Rick Steves is a well-known travel expert, and his engaging commentary will give you a deeper understanding of the art, architecture, and history of Florence.

I used this app when I visited the Uffizi and found it to be incredibly informative and easy to follow. Instead of standing in long lines for a group tour, I could enjoy the art at my own pace, pausing whenever I wanted to take a closer look or snap a photo.

Pro Tip: If you're traveling with family or in a group, this app lets everyone enjoy the tour independently, so you won't feel rushed or bored if someone wants to linger longer at a specific painting.

4. Moovit:

Florence is a city best explored on foot, but there are times when you'll need to hop on a bus or tram to reach further destinations like Fiesole or the outskirts of the city. Moovit is your go-to app for public transportation in Florence. It provides real-time schedules, route information, and even step-by-step directions on how to get from one place to another.

On one occasion, I was headed to the Bardini Gardens, a beautiful spot on a hill with fantastic views of the city. I wasn't quite sure how to get there, but Moovit guided me through a bus transfer with ease, making it hassle-free.

Pro Tip: The app works in multiple languages and is perfect for navigating Florence's public transport system, especially if you're unfamiliar with the routes. It's especially handy for longer trips or excursions to nearby attractions.

5. Firenze Card:
If you plan on visiting several major attractions in Florence, the **Firenze Card** app is a must. It provides you with an entry ticket that grants access to 72 museums and attractions in the city, including the Uffizi Gallery, the Pitti Palace, and the Bargello Museum. The card also lets you skip most of the lines, which can save you hours during peak seasons.

I had the Firenze Card during my last visit and was able to breeze past long queues at the Duomo and the Accademia Gallery. It allowed me to maximize my time in the city, rather than wasting it standing in line.

Pro Tip: You can buy the card directly through the app, and it works for 72 hours from the first use, so you can pace yourself without feeling rushed to see everything in a single day.

6. Florence's Official Tourist Guide:
For an all-around resource, the **Florence Official Tourist Guide** app gives you comprehensive information on the city's attractions, events, and even lesser-known spots. It includes maps, suggested itineraries, and tips on where to find the best gelato or where to see live music.

I used this app to discover the **Museum of San Salvi**, an off-the-beaten-path gem that I would have missed without its helpful recommendations. The app is easy to navigate and lets you explore Florence with an insider's perspective.

Pro Tip: The app includes up-to-date event listings, so if you're looking for festivals, exhibitions, or concerts while in Florence, it's an excellent resource to check.

Florence's Art Movements and Influences

From the stunning frescoes on church walls to the marble statues that define the city's skyline, Florence's art movements have shaped both Western art and global culture for centuries. Whether you're wandering through its museums or simply strolling down cobbled streets, the legacy of Florence's artistic heritage is impossible to miss.

The Birth of the Renaissance
The story of Florence's art begins with the dawn of the **Renaissance** in the late 14th century. This was a period of great cultural rebirth after the Middle Ages, and Florence became the epicenter of this revolution. Artists and thinkers, like **Leonardo da Vinci**, **Michelangelo**, and **Sandro Botticelli**, found inspiration here, transforming how people viewed the world and themselves.

One of the most visible signs of Florence's Renaissance influence is the **Duomo** (Cathedral of Santa Maria del Fiore), with its breathtaking dome designed by Filippo Brunelleschi. When Brunelleschi created this architectural marvel, he didn't just build a church; he changed the course of Western architecture. Walking through Florence today, you can see how the Renaissance turned art from medieval religious iconography into an exploration of human experience and natural beauty.

The Medici Family:
No discussion of Florence's art history would be complete without mentioning the **Medici family**. This powerful banking dynasty had a profound influence on the city's development and was crucial in supporting artists, architects, and scholars during the Renaissance.

The Medici were not just wealthy; they were intellectuals and art lovers. Cosimo de' Medici, the patriarch, famously supported artists like **Donatello**, whose statues — such as his bronze **David** — were groundbreaking for their realism. Meanwhile, **Lorenzo de' Medici**, known as "Lorenzo the Magnificent," played a key role in the rise of **Botticelli** and **Michelangelo**. The Medici's patronage helped Florence become a global center for the arts, and today, many of the city's most famous works, such as Botticelli's **The Birth of Venus** (now at the Uffizi Gallery), remain as testaments to their impact.

Mannerism:
As the Renaissance began to wane, a new movement emerged in Florence known as **Mannerism**. While the Renaissance focused on harmony, balance,

and proportion, Mannerism deliberately departed from these ideals. The style was characterized by elongated figures, exaggerated poses, and a sense of emotional tension, offering a more complex and often ambiguous portrayal of the human condition.

One of the most famous examples of Mannerist art in Florence is **Pontormo's** *Entombment of Christ*, housed in the **Church of Santa Felicita**. The figures in this painting appear contorted, as if caught in an emotional, almost surreal moment, which was a sharp contrast to the calm and balanced compositions of the earlier Renaissance. Mannerism's influence can still be seen in modern art, especially in its more experimental approaches to form and expression.

Baroque Influence and Beyond

After the Renaissance and Mannerism, Florence also experienced the Baroque period in the 17th century, a time when art became more dramatic, emotional, and detailed. During this period, artists like **Caravaggio** and **Gian Lorenzo Bernini** captured the human experience with intense realism and dramatic contrasts of light and shadow. In Florence, the **Basilica of San Lorenzo** and its interior, decorated by **Giorgio Vasari** and **Francesco Salviati**, provide a taste of the grandeur and opulence typical of the Baroque period.

Modern Art in Florence

While Florence is most famous for its Renaissance treasures, its art scene has continued to evolve. The **20th century** brought a surge of modern art movements that challenged classical traditions. Artists like **Amedeo Modigliani**, whose works reflect both emotion and experimentation, contributed to Florence's vibrant modern art scene. Today, Florence still offers a platform for contemporary art, with numerous galleries and exhibitions dedicated to both Italian and international artists.

One place to experience this blend of old and new is the **Museo Novecento**, a contemporary art museum in the heart of Florence. It celebrates the city's ongoing relationship with the arts while maintaining its roots in the Renaissance traditions that made Florence world-renowned.

Real-World Example:
The **Uffizi Gallery** is a perfect place to see firsthand how Florence's art movements evolved over time. Located in a grand Renaissance building, the gallery houses some of the most iconic works of the Renaissance, including **Michelangelo's** *Doni Tondo* and **Botticelli's** *Primavera*. But visitors will also find examples from later movements like Mannerism and Baroque. Walking through its rooms is like taking a chronological journey through Florence's history, and it's an excellent spot to appreciate the city's art movements in context.

Personal Anecdote:
On my first visit to Florence, I remember being struck not just by the famous masterpieces but also by the energy in the city's streets. The Medici family's legacy isn't just in the museums; it's alive in the city's architecture, public spaces, and the people who still live in the heart of this artistic treasure trove. I'll never forget sitting in Piazza della Signoria, surrounded by sculptures, and feeling like I was part of something much larger than just the present day. It's an experience that reminds you how deeply art runs through the veins of this city.

Recommended Books and Films about Florence

If you're planning a trip to this stunning Italian city, immersing yourself in its cultural and historical background through literature and cinema can enhance your experience and deepen your understanding of the city. Below are some must-read books and must-see films that will transport you to Florence, whether you're at home planning your trip or already strolling its cobblestone streets.

Books about Florence
1. **"The Birth of Venus" by Sarah Dunant**
   Set in 15th-century Florence during the rise of the Renaissance, *The*

Birth of Venus is a captivating historical novel that brings the city to life. The story centers on the life of a young woman, Alessandra, caught in the turbulence of political intrigue, religious reform, and personal desire. Dunant's detailed descriptions of Florence's art, architecture, and societal pressures allow readers to feel as though they are walking the streets of the city.

Personal anecdote: When I read this novel before my trip, it gave me a deeper appreciation for the history behind Florence's art and the tensions that shaped its cultural development. I found myself looking at the paintings in the Uffizi Gallery through a more informed lens, especially Botticelli's *The Birth of Venus*, which comes alive through Dunant's storytelling.

2. **"In the Footsteps of the Medici" by Paul Strathern**
   The Medici family is inextricably linked to Florence, so a book about them is a great way to understand the city's fascinating history. *In the Footsteps of the Medici* explores the lives of this powerful family, whose influence shaped Florence's politics, art, and culture. Strathern does an excellent job of combining biography with history, making it easy to follow the Medici's rise to power and their cultural legacy.
   Personal tip: This book is perfect to read before visiting the Medici Villas or the Palazzo Medici Riccardi, as it provides historical context that will make your visit more engaging.

3. **"Florence: The Paintings & Frescoes" by Ross King**
   For those interested in art, this book is a comprehensive guide to Florence's stunning paintings and frescoes, including works by Michelangelo, Raphael, and Leonardo da Vinci. King, a well-known art historian, does an excellent job of telling the stories behind these masterpieces, making it easy to understand their significance in the context of the Renaissance.
   Real-life example: I found this book invaluable when I visited the Galleria dell'Accademia and saw Michelangelo's *David*. The insights from King's book allowed me to appreciate the grandeur of the sculpture in a

new light, seeing it as more than just a piece of art but as a symbol of Florence's dominance during the Renaissance.

Films About Florence

1. **"A Room with a View" (1985)**
   Directed by James Ivory, this film adaptation of E.M. Forster's novel is one of the best depictions of Florence's romantic allure. The story follows a young English woman, Lucy Honeychurch, as she travels to Florence and becomes caught in a love triangle that changes her life. The film showcases Florence's beautiful landscapes, from the iconic Ponte Vecchio to the serene countryside.
   Personal anecdote: Watching this movie before my trip inspired me to visit many of the locations featured in the film, including the enchanting Boboli Gardens and the Palazzo Pitti. It felt like stepping into the past and experiencing Florence's charm in the same way Lucy did.

2. **"The Talented Mr. Ripley" (1999)**
   Based on Patricia Highsmith's novel, *The Talented Mr. Ripley* is a psychological thriller set in Italy, with several key scenes filmed in Florence. The film stars Matt Damon as Tom Ripley, a young man who becomes involved in a web of deceit and murder while traveling through Europe. Florence serves as the perfect backdrop for the film's tense atmosphere, with its beautiful yet sometimes ominous streets.
   Tip: While in Florence, you can trace Ripley's steps by visiting some of the city's iconic landmarks, like the Piazza della Signoria or the Uffizi Gallery, where the film's climactic scene takes place.

3. **"Inferno" (2016)**
   Directed by Ron Howard and based on the Dan Brown novel, *Inferno* is a fast-paced thriller that takes viewers on a journey through Florence. The story follows Robert Langdon (played by Tom Hanks) as he solves a mystery related to Dante Alighieri's *Divine Comedy*. The film highlights some of Florence's most iconic locations, including the Duomo, the

Palazzo Vecchio, and the Boboli Gardens.
Personal anecdote: If you're a fan of thrillers and art history, this film is an exciting way to explore Florence through a different lens. I watched *Inferno* right before a visit to the Palazzo Vecchio and was able to recognize many of the film's locations firsthand.

Bonus Resources for Florence Fans

For those who want to delve even deeper into Florence's cultural history, there are a few more books and films worth exploring:

- **Books:**
  "*The Florentine Renaissance: A History*" by Richard C. Trexler is a scholarly yet accessible book that examines Florence's golden age of art, politics, and society.
- **Films:**
  "*The Birth of Venus*" (2003) is a lesser-known Italian film based on the novel by Sarah Dunant, bringing the story of the Medici and Florence's artistic revolution to life on screen.

Conclusion

Florence is not just a city you visit; it's an experience that lingers long after you've returned home. With every step along its cobbled streets, every gaze at its iconic landmarks, and every bite of its exquisite cuisine, you'll find yourself falling deeper in love with its charm. Florence invites you to slow down, immerse yourself in its Renaissance beauty, and connect with its soul—a place where history, art, and culture come alive in ways that feel both timeless and personal.

As you navigate Florence, don't just stick to the guidebook favorites. While landmarks like the Duomo and the Uffizi are must-sees, the magic of Florence often lies in the unexpected. Venture into the quiet alleys of the Oltrarno district, where artisans pour their hearts into centuries-old crafts. Wander through hidden gardens that offer a serene escape from the city's bustle. Stop by a tiny trattoria, and you might discover your favorite meal of the trip. Florence rewards those who explore with curiosity and an open heart.

Take time to savor the little things—a morning espresso in a bustling piazza, the golden glow of the Arno River at sunset, or the echo of footsteps in a centuries-old church. Florence teaches you to appreciate life's details, reminding you that even in the busiest moments, beauty is all around.

Practically speaking, Florence is a city best experienced on foot. Wear comfortable shoes, carry a reusable water bottle, and be prepared to get pleasantly lost. It's in those unplanned detours that you'll stumble upon a quiet courtyard or a lively local market. And don't shy away from asking for recommendations; Florentines are proud of their city and often eager to share its treasures.

Most importantly, let Florence inspire you. Whether it's the art that pushes you to create, the history that sparks your curiosity, or the food that warms your soul, this city has a way of leaving a mark on everyone who visits. As you leave Florence, you'll carry its stories and spirit with you—a reminder of the beauty that exists when passion and tradition meet.

So pack your bags, bring your sense of wonder, and get ready for a journey that will not just fill your travel journal but enrich your heart. Florence is waiting for you—are you ready to embrace its timeless allure?

Printed in Great Britain
by Amazon